What The U. S. Military Can Do To Defeat Terrorism

WHAT THE U. S. MILITARY CAN DO TO DEFEAT TERRORISM

Joseph W. Graham, Ph. D.

Writers Club Press
San Jose New York Lincoln Shanghai

What The U. S. Military Can Do To Defeat Terrorism

Writers Club Press
an imprint of iUniverse, Inc.

For information address:
iUniverse, Inc.
5220 S. 16th St., Suite 200
Lincoln, NE 68512
www.iuniverse.com

ISBN: 0-595-22259-5

Printed in the United States of America

For My Wife, Sandra

My life, My love

Contents

Introduction ix

Chapter I 1

The Development and Growth of the United States Military Operational
Strategy from 1968–2002.

Chapter 2 47

What Leading Experts of Military Strategy Say About Center of Gravity

Chapter 3 53

How the Center of Gravity was applied to the Gulf War, Panama Invasion,
Somalia Operation, and is being applied to our current war on terrorism

Chapter 4 81

Summary

About the Author 83

Introduction

"One must keep the dominant characteristics of both belligerents in mind. Out of these characteristics a certain center of gravity develops, the hub of all power and movement, on which everything depends. That is the point against which all our energies should be directed."

—Carl von Clausewitz

This book traces the development and growth of the United States Military Operational Strategy and how its newest concept 'Center of Gravity' can be applied to defeat terrorism. Because the National Military Strategy changed 180 degrees from what it was during the Cold War, from containment of the Soviet threat to supporting an engagement and enlargement strategy, it has caused confusion about the new strategy among the U.S. Military and therefore the Services should develop a universally basic concept of Center of Gravity in fighting campaigns. Terrorism is the new paradigm in the world that falls under the engagement and enlargement strategy. That which was once theorized has now become our reality. Like many other realities that the Military face, it must deal with terrorism based upon past measures used to solve problems. The Military rely on a proven set of measures that help to analyze and break a problem down in order to determine where it can be impacted the most in order to be resolved. There are many authorities that confess to know what route to take to defeat terrorism and terrorists. They spout their solutions to the problem in 30-second sound bites on television. These off the cuff analysis do not address the details needed to understand how to solve the problem of terrorism. A carefully analysis of the center of gravity of terrorism must be done to identify those critical factors that will eliminate the problem we now face. Chapter 1 shows the development and growth of the United States Military Operational Strategy from 1968–2002. Chapter 2 compare and contrast points of views of leading experts of Military Strategy about Center of Gravity. Chapter 3 examines how Center of Gravity was applied to the , Gulf War, Panama Invasion, Somalia Operation, and is being applied to our current war on terrorism.

Chapter I

The Development and Growth of the United States Military Operational Strategy from 1968–2002.

Since the end of the cold war, there is broad-based sentiment that the United States has lost its guiding principles that ensures its freedom – deterrence and containment. The Bush administration foreign policies moves initially seem to favor isolationism, leaving other countries to solve their own problems. For example, asked a question during the October 3, 2000 debates that if President Milosevic of Yugoslavia refuses to leave office, what action, if any, should the United States take to get him out of there? Governor Bush replied No. It's not in our national interest to use force. I would use pressure and diplomacy. There is a difference what the president did in Kosovo and this. It's up to the people in this region to take control of their country. If it's in our vital national interest, and that means whether our territory is threatened or people could be harmed, whether or not the alliances are—our defense alliances are threatened, whether or not our friends in the Middle East are threatened. That would be a time to seriously consider the use of force. Secondly, whether or not the mission was clear. Whether or not it was a clear understanding as to what the mission would be. Thirdly, whether or not we were prepared and trained to win. Whether or not our forces were of high morale and high standing and well-equipped. And finally, whether or not there was an exit strategy. I would take the use of force very seriously. I would be guarded in my approach. I don't think we can be all things to all people in the world. I think we've got to be very careful when we commit our troops.[1]

In a later debate on October 17, 2000, Candidate Bush stated "I'm concerned that we're overdeployed around the world. See, I think the mission has somewhat become fuzzy. Should I be fortunate enough to earn your confidence, the mission of the United States military will be to be prepared and ready to fight and win war. And therefore prevent war from happening in the first place. There may be some moments when we use our troops as peacekeepers, but not often. The Vice President mentioned my view of long-term for the military. I want to make sure the equipment for our military is the best it can possibly be, of course. But we have an opportunity to use our research and development capacities, the great technology of the United States, to make our military lighter, harder to find, more lethal. We have an opportunity, really, if you think about it, if we're smart and have got a strategic vision and a leader who understands strategic planning, to make sure that we change the terms of the battlefield of the future so we can keep the peace. This is a peaceful

---

[1] Debate Transcripts October 3, 2000.

nation, and I intend to keep the peace."[2] Indeed, soon after his election last year, President George W. Bush asked his defense secretary Donald Rumsfeld to "challenge the status quo inside the Pentagon and to develop a United States strategy necessary to have a force equipped for warfare of the 21st century". If the details of the Pentagon's new strategic blueprint are not yet clear, it is, however, possible to describe its underlying principles.

The strategic blueprint being developed by the Bush administration will rest on three fundamental precepts: America-centrism, meaning that any deployment of US military forces abroad—whether or not in conjunction with US allies—must above all serve American interests; global reach, i.e. the ability to project US military power to any point on the globe, at any time and under any circumstances; and perpetual supremacy, meaning the application of science, technology and money to ensure that US forces and weapons will always be superior to those of all other nations. These are not, of course, entirely new ideas. Other US administrations have favored one or other of these principles. But never have these precepts been articulated with such consistency and fervor - to the point that they represent a new and important departure in American strategic thinking. US military policy, like that of any nation, has always been based on the premise that the employment of US forces abroad must serve fundamental American security interests. But US interests also included the pursuit of other, more lofty objectives—the defense of democracy against the spread of totalitarianism, cohesion of the Western alliance system, preservation of regional stability and so on. These objectives have not entirely disappeared under Bush, but they are being pushed aside by an explicit emphasis on the pursuit of America's own national interests. US leaders argue that the West no longer faces

---

[2] Debate Transcript October 17, 2000.

an overarching threat like that once posed by the Soviet Union, so there is no compelling reason for Washington to subordinate its national interests to the common defense. "America must be involved in the world," Bush declared in 1999. "But that does not mean that our military is the answer to every difficult foreign policy situation." Rather, he argued, the use of force by the US must be governed by a National Military Strategy that emphasizes "enduring national interests"[3]

What is this National Military Strategy? Most of us grew up in a world that was consumed by the Cold War. The strategy at that point in time was containment of the Soviet threat. The Threat determined how we did things, how we wrote doctrine, did our training, modernize, and explained the importance of the United States Military. There was a real threat out there and we could identify it, and we understood it. All one had to do was to go to the border between East and West Germany and you understood the nature of the threat. If one went to the Berlin Wall, he understood there were two ways of life that were involved in a fundamental struggle. When the Cold War ended, the United States Military found themselves in a different world. Some have referred to it as a New World Order. Simply said, it was long on new and short on order. The military found itself trying to adjust to a situation that it was not prepared for and did not, quite frankly, understand. So when one talks about readiness and change today, he must talk about readiness for what—and that means understanding the National Military Strategy because it's a strategy designed for a world that is very different from the one of a few short years ago. The National Military Strategy changed from containment of the Soviet threat to supporting an engagement and enlargement strategy. As stated before, this is a 180 degrees approach from what it was during the Cold War. Engagement and

---

[3] Klare, Michael T. (2001, July) American Military Revolution. Le Monde diplomatique.

enlargement meant that to achieve a National Military Strategy, certain goals had to be achieved. Those goals rests on three pillars: to be able to "respond" to a crisis anywhere in the world or anywhere the vital interests of the United States are threatened; to be able to "shape" the environment—to make the world safer for our children and grandchildren: and at the same time to be able to "prepare" for an uncertain future - to be able to change the Army in a very fundamental way to meet the asymmetrical threats that we will face in the future and to adjust to the world that is changing very rapidly. And so the National Military Strategy is built upon those three pillars: to be able to respond, to be able to shape and to be able to prepare for the future. The Army has to be ready to perform missions that support all three of those pillars. [4]

With the change in strategy and the pillars that support it, the end of the cold war dispelled other assumptions. American strategists no longer expect to fight a massive, protracted ground war in central Europe or any other location. The military expect to fight short but intense campaigns in widely scattered locations across the world. Because the US cannot afford to station large numbers of heavy weapons in every region of the world, the US must be able to transport its forces and equipment rapidly from bases in the US. This is not entirely new. But most of the weapons now in the Pentagon inventory were developed during the cold war era and are difficult to transport. The problem that this poses became evident with the war in Kosovo: the US army experienced great difficulty in moving its heavy equipment. After the war many American strategists expressed deep concern about this. Under President Bush the redesign of American combat forces for easy and rapid transportation to distant battle zones has been a

---

[4] Reimer, Dennis J. (1999, March) Remarks to Reserve Officer Association: The Army a Year of Transition. Chief of Staff Army in Transition. www.dtic.mil/armylink/news/mar1999/s1990302csaspeec.html

major priority. For the army, this means breaking up large armored units into smaller, more mobile detachments. To compensate for their smaller size, these detachments will be provided with large numbers of precision-guided munitions (PGMs). Similarly, for the navy, there has been less emphasis on large surface warships such as aircraft carriers, and more on small, stealthy ships equipped with guided missiles of all types. The air force has faced the fewest changes under this plan, as it is already capable of moving its aircraft around the world at short notice. But it will acquire more aerial refueling aircraft and long-range cargo planes. In all, as Bush declared on 13 February, "On land, our heavy forces will be lighter, our light forces will be more lethal. They will be easier to deploy and to sustain. In the air, we will be able to strike across the world with pinpoint accuracy. On the oceans, we will connect information and weapons in new ways, maximizing our ability to project power onto land". All this, Bush said, will require "great effort and new spending". It is anathema to entrenched military and industrial interests. The administration is, however, determined to enhance the US' capacity to fight and prevail on any conceivable battlefield, especially in East Asia. [5] Some view this as the reason that the terrorist attacked the United States. As our nation learned after World War I, we can find no security for America in isolationism nor prosperity in protectionism. For the American people to be safer and enjoy expanding opportunities, the nation must work to deter would-be aggressors, open foreign markets, promote the spread of democracy a broad, combat transnational dangers of terrorism, drug trafficking and international crime, encourage sustainable development and pursue new opportunities for peace.

As addressed in the 1996 National Security Strategy, American national security strategy was therefore based on enlarging the community of market democracies while deterring and limiting a range of

---

[5] Klare, Michael, (2001, July). America's Military Revolution.

threats to the nation, allies and its interests. The more that democracy and political and economic liberalization take hold in the world, particularly in countries of strategic importance, the safer the nation is likely to be and the more the people are likely to prosper. [6] Regardless of the reason, to solve the problem one must identify the underpinnings of international crime and terrorism to determine its center of gravity, decision points, and vulnerability to successfully solve the problem. In particular, the U. S. Military must develop a universally accepted Joint understanding of center of gravity in order to defeat terrorism.

An examination of center of gravity is fast becoming the cornerstone of war fighting doctrine. In several magazine articles and television briefings , one can hear center of gravity being used to describe how to defeat terrorism. The nature of center of gravity is linked to the evolution of U.S. Army doctrine. Therefore one must look at the historical factors that shaped the concept of center of gravity. After Vietnam, the U.S. Army began to refocus operations based upon the importance of mass in order to defeat large land forces such as the Soviet Union. This marked a turning point in military thinking and led to the development of Field Manual 100-5, Operations. It was the first edition in a series of key documents that would guide the evolution of warfare that has led to center of gravity. FM 100-5 began in 1976 and centered on what was called Active Defense, which focused on a dominating defense and overcoming an enemy with massive firepower. This method was based upon the combination of a flexible resistance (to slow, weaken, and eventually halt enemy attacks) with localized counterattacks meant to throw the enemy off balance, and eventually force his retreat. In the 1982, FM 100-5 advanced to the concept of Airland Battle, emphasized the use of strongpoints held by infantry and anti-tank forces to channel

---

[6] (1996, February). National Security Strategy. The Whtie House.

enemy attacks into main battle areas. Ideally, counteracttacks would be aimed against the flanks of the enemy force. [7] Identification of center of gravity as we know it today received little attention during this period. Maneuver was king and it also contains a long-range attritional element (Follow-On Forces Attack), the maneuver dimension of Air-Land Battle doctrine owes much to the classic lessons of armored warfare. It's goal is to disrupt the enemy's ability to fight rather than to destroy his forces cumulatively. Surprise blows against forces and facilities in critical sectors are meant to dislocate the enemy's plans and dispositions, and ideally the entire functioning of his chain of command. FM 100-5, Operations, emphasizes initiative, depth, agility, synchronization, maneuver, firepower, protection, and leadership. Initiative is defined as the ability to take advantage throughout the entire operational zone, to prevent the enemy from freely concentrating his firepower or maneuvering his forces. Agility is the ability to change plans, operational direction and tactics quickly and with minimal disruption, and is achieved by a flexible organizational structure, as well as by commanders who can decide and act quickly, improvising as needed. Synchronization requires a unity of purpose in the action of all elements involved in an operation. Maneuver is movement designed to achieve concentration, surprise, shock, and momentum. Firepower implies the concentration of fire against critical points in the enemy's deployment to suppress his own fire, neutralize his tactics, and generally destroy his ability to fight. Protection is the converse of firepower: U.S. forces must be shielded from enemy fire to preserve their own freedom of maneuver. It includes the use of cover, deception, concealment, suppression, and mobility. Finally, leadership is described as the crucial element; to implement Air-Land Battle methods, leaders must plan and act on their own initiative within the general concept of the operation, while inspiring their

---

[7] Dictionary of Modern War, Luttwak, Kohel, p. 4

troops. The adoption of maneuver-based doctrine by the U.S. Military reflected its sense of material weakness as compared with the Soviet Union during this time period. But the military's continuing centralization of command and control and ingrained habits of tactical micromanagement by higher echelons were serious obstacles to a full application of Air-Land Battle doctrine. The collision between the new doctrine and traditional preferences is reflected in the divisional organization that was adopted at the same time as Air-Land Battle; instead of smaller, leaner, and more numerous units, the new divisions are still very large and unwieldy. Moreover, the U.S. Army's equipment bureaucracy remained focused on weapons designed to fight an attritional war.[8] Within the joint battle area, air and ground forces concentrate major combat power, engage in fire and maneuver, fire support, special operations, close air support, and defensive counter air interdiction. This is normally the enemy's operational center of gravity where the "decisive operations" that will bring about the total and violent destruction of his forces will occur. Inside the staging area, air, ground and sea forces perform security missions but are concerned primarily with logistical, basing, airlift and deployment concerns. As the military establishment reduces in size and continues with its transition from forward defense to forward presence (power projection), it becomes increasingly important for all the services to agree on the evolution of common doctrine to successfully operate across the continuum of military operations.[9]

There was little discussion about center of gravity, but Air-land Battle provided the link to the evolution common doctrine and center

---

[8] Dictionary of Modern War, Luttwalk, Koehl, p. 18.

[9] Steinke (1990, Spring). Joint strategic operational approach to meeting the NSC challenge's in 1990s. Parameters. U.S. Army War College Quarterly.

of gravity. As technological advances continued to emerge, it became apparent that there needed to be a concept that covered the entire depth of the battlefield. In 1986, FM 100-5 provided the critical link where the military began to look at operations from three levels of war, the strategic, the operational, and the tactical. The focus of the operational level was stated as "the employment of military forces to achieve strategic goals". This linked tactics to strategy. Section 603 of the Goldwater-Nichols Defense Department Reorganization Act of 1986, elaborates a national security strategy that was tailored for this new era and builds upon America's unmatched strengths. Focusing on new threats and new opportunities, its central goals are:

> To enhance our society with military forces that are ready to fight with effective representation abroad.

> To bolster America's economic revitalization.

> To promote democracy abroad.

President Clinton stated that his Administration had worked diligently to pursue these central goals. The national security strategy report presented the strategy that has guided the effort. It was premised on a belief that the line between domestic and foreign policies were disappearing—that America must revitalize its economy if it were to sustain military forces, foreign initiatives and global influence, and that America must engage actively abroad if we are to open foreign markets and create jobs. He believed that the goals of enhancing our security, bolstering our economic prosperity and promoting democracy are mutually supportive. Secure nations are more likely to support free trade and maintain democratic structures. Free market nations with growing economies and strong and open trade ties are more likely to feel secure and to work toward freedom. Also, democratic states are less likely to threaten

America's interests and more likely to cooperate with the United States to meet security threats and promote free trade and sustainable development. These goals were supported by ensuring America remains engaged in the world and by enlarging the community of secure, free market and democratic nations. As the boundaries between threats that start outside our borders and the challenges from within are diminishing, the problems others face today can more quickly become ours, tomorrow. This is why U.S. leadership and engagement have never been more important: if the U.S. withdraws from this world today, our citizens will have to pay the price of our neglect. Therefore, one simple standard measurement of success of our efforts abroad must be addressed: Have we made the lives of the American people safer, today; have we made tomorrow better and more secure for our children?[10]

To support this standard of measurement of success, major theater land campaigns needed to emphasize Air-Land operations and involve operations against an enemy in depth, although such operations will in many cases be nonlinear and dynamic, placing additional demands on joint coordination and creating additional opportunities for employment of joint forces in a variety of settings, as specified in the theater plan. The typical theater campaign plan segregates Air-Land Operations into three major divisions: the forward area known as the "joint intelligence and air attack area"; the joint battle area; and the joint staging and dispersal area. All the services will, by doctrine, have some degree of responsibility for activities within each area; however, Army Air-Land doctrine envisions most of the activity in the forward area and the joint battle area as being primarily an Army and Air Force effort.[11] In 1993, FM 100-5 focused on post-Cold War operations, which focused on integrated destruction of enemy forces in depth.

[10] 1996 National Security Strategy.
[11] Steike (1990, Spring). Joint strategic operations approach to meeting NSC needs to the 1990s. Parameters. U.S. Army War College Quarterly.

During the Gulf War, this concept was further cemented as operational doctrine by the overwhelming defeat of the Iraqi forces. The theory of center of gravity is rooted in operations conducted during the Gulf War and evolved into geometric and linear thinking. Asymmetrical Force, Parallel Operations, time and physics have overtaken the traditional force-on-force model of attrition warfare, geared to battle lines on the ground, massed forces, and sequential operations. Strategies of the future will be oriented less toward territory lost or gained and more toward eliminating the enemy's ability to wage war. Future operations will emphasize asymmetrical force, applied intensely and overwhelmingly against the enemy's strategic, operational, and tactical "centers of gravity," including his order of battle and supporting infrastructure. These targets must be attacked "in parallel"—all of them concurrently—rather than by serial attacks that present the adversary with an opportunity to adjust, adapt, or mount a counteroffensive. Critical "center of gravity" targets will generally lie deep in the enemy's territory and will be protected by lethal defenses and other means.

Frequently, they will be located in urban areas. For reasons that include the penetration of hostile airspace, success of the attack, the avoidance of collateral damage, and the limitation of casualties on both sides, the force of choice will be deep-strike aircraft employing stealth and precision-guided munitions.[12]

Military Field Manual 100-5, Operations, and Clausewitz defines center of gravity as "the hub of **all power** and movement upon which everything depends". FM 100-5 further states that mass of the enemy army, the enemy's battle command structure, public opinion, national will, and all alliance or coalition structure defines a nations center of gravity and thus its national power. National Power is based upon Strategic

[12] Correll, John T. (1996). AFA 1996-97 Statement of Policy: Aerospace Power Makes the Difference. Journal of the Air Force Association.

Geometry of four pillars; Political & Diplomatic, Economic, Informational/technological, and Military. By bringing each of these pillars to bare, a country can defeat enemy forces, rather they are strategic, operational, or tactical. FM 100-5 describes operational art as "...the skillful employment of military forces to attain strategic and/or operational objectives in a theater of operations through the design, organization, integration, and conduct of theater strategies, campaigns, major operations, and battles. Operational art translates theater strategy and design into operational design which links and integrates the tactical battles and engagements that, when fought and won, achieve the strategic aim." Operational art links tactical events to strategic objectives. Using operational art, the Commander-in-Charge (CINC) envisions the theater strategic and operational design. To achieve theater strategic design and objectives, the CINC arranges unified operations, joint operations, major operations, and tactical-level battles. Operational art at the operational level uses major operations in support of joint campaigns to sequence these events over time and space. Senior army commanders and their staffs practicing operational art may operate in a joint and possibly combined arena. They sequence Army operations to achieve theater strategic and operational objectives.

The theater strategic and operational concepts that explain operational art and design include center of gravity, decisive points, lines of operation, culminating point, indirect approach, positional advantage and strategic concentration of forces, and deception. The CINC and his principal subordinates should agree on what design features are most important to accomplishing the mission. The CINC establishes the first use and priority of these concepts. Subordinates' use and priority is a subset of the CINC's. For example, the CINC selects the strategic center of gravity, and subordinates select decisive points on the path to attacking the center of gravity.

The essence of operational art is concentrating friendly military forces and resources against the enemy's main sources of strength (strategic center of gravity) in a manner that provides the Joint Forces Commander (JFC) with the strategic and operational advantage and the initiative. The destruction, dislocation, or neutralization of the enemy center of gravity should prove decisive in achieving strategic objectives. Similarly, the JFC must identify the theater friendly center of gravity and protect it. The enemy center of gravity exists at all levels of war. A center of gravity is the foundation of capability—what von Clausewitz called "the hub of all power and movement, on which everything depends...the point at which all our energies should be directed." Joint Publications 3-0 also states that centers of gravity are the foundation of capability. They are those characteristics, capabilities, or resources of power from which a military force derives its freedom of action, physical strength, or will to fight.[13] The center of gravity may be seen in more complex components or abstract terms, such as the enemy's alliance, solidarity, or national will and in actual examples such as strategic reserves, C^2, logistics, industrial base, public support, a set of critical functions, or national strategy itself. The center of gravity is most useful at the operational level of war as an analytical tool to focus the effort against the enemy's strength while designing campaigns and operations to assist commanders and staffs in analyzing friendly and adversary sources of strength as well as weaknesses and vulnerabilities. Analysis of centers of gravity, both adversary and friendly, is a continuous process throughout an operation. Destruction or neutralization of adversary centers of gravity is the most direct path to victory. However, centers of gravity can change during the course of an operation and, at any given time, centers of gravity may not be apparent or readily discernible. Identification of

13 JP 3-0, Chp 3, p III-22.

adversary centers of gravity require detailed knowledge and understanding of how opponents organize, fight, and make decisions as well as their physical and psychological strengths and weaknesses. One must know the circumstances that may cause centers of gravity to change and should adjust friendly operations accordingly. Adversary centers of gravity frequently will be well protected, making direct attack difficult and costly. Indirect attacks can be used against centers of gravity until favorable conditions allow successful direct attacks. Friendly centers of gravity are also important to identify so they can be protected.[14] In Military Operations Other Than War (MOOTW) such as disaster relief and humanitarian assistance the enemy's center of gravity is the threat of hunger or the elements of the environment. The uniqueness of these operations requires the commander and his staff to understand the military's role in relation to the total efforts of national power being used to resolve the situation. The military's role supports the other elements of national power.

Decisive points provide commanders with a significant advantage. They are the keys to defeating or protecting the center of gravity. Normally, there are more decisive points in a theater than there are resources to attack them. Decisive points are usually geographic in nature, such as a constricted sea lane, a hill, a town, or an air base and could include other elements such as command posts, critical boundaries, airspace, or communications and/or intelligence nodes. In some cases, specific key events also may be decisive points , such as attainment of air or naval superiority or commitment of the adversary's reserve. In other cases, decisive points may be systemic, such as command and control systems and refueling or ammunition storage capability. Decisive are

---

14 JP 3-0, p. III-22-23.

not centers of gravity; they are keys to attacking protected centers of gravity. The commander designates the most critical points and objectives as a means of gaining freedom of maneuver to gain and maintain momentum. By correctly identifying and then attacking (or protecting) decisive points, the commander is able to defeat the enemy's center of gravity. Decisive points serve as trigger points for friendly force actions that sustain the initiative. The area of operation (AO) will have more decisive points than available resources to commit against them. The commander and his staff must conduct a risk analysis to prioritize the friendly force efforts. A stand-alone, individual information war action can be decisive. Winning the information battle before the war can be even more decisive than winning it during hostilities. Winning the information war before the war may preclude combat operations. The ability to get inside an adversary's decision-making cycle (his operational ability to react) is critical to attacking his centers of gravity, exploiting his weaknesses, and effectively concentrating our own combat power. An area that must not be overlooked is using, and even driving, emerging technologies to access the tactical situation on the ground. Lines of operation define the directional orientation of a force in relation to the enemy. They connect the force with its base of operations—from which it receives reinforcements and resupply—and its forward units—where it operates against the enemy. This concept is linked to the interior or exterior (or combination) directional orientation of a force in relation to the enemy. Lines of operation are used to focus combat power effects toward a desired end.

The culminating point is the point in time and space at which the offensive becomes overextended, and offensive combat power no longer sufficiently exceeds that of the defender to allow continuation of the offense. While this point may not be precisely determined, the commander and his staff should consider it in the design concept. A defensive culminating point is that point at which the defender's capability is reduced to such a degree that continued pursuit could result in the defender's defeat in detail. If the defender's aim is to transition to the attack, then the culminating point is where the defender must revert to a holding action and await reinforcement; If the defender's aim is to retain terrain, then the culminating point is where the defender must withdraw, delay, and so forth.

An indirect approach is a scheme that attacks the enemy center of gravity from unexpected directions or at unexpected times. The indirect approach seeks enemy vulnerabilities and avoids enemy strengths. The application of techniques to win the information war is one area that leads itself to the indirect approach. When possible, JFCs attack enemy centers of gravity directly. Where direct attack means attacking into an opponent's strength, JFCs should seek an indirect approach. Examples include attacks of flanks, rear areas, or C^2 capabilities.

Vulnerabilities are boundaries or seams between forces, the relative weaknesses of unprotected flanks or rear areas, or unhardened command, control, communications, and intelligence (C3I) facilities. Positional Advantage and Strategic Concentration of Forces Strategic realities indicate that force ratios may not favor friendly forces across the theater. Therefore, the JFC determines where to strategically concentrate force and in what areas to accept risk. Clearly, this aspect ties in with the center of gravity, indirect approach, positional advantage, and deception. Joint forces seek to obtain positional advantage relative to enemy forces. Such advantage includes control of territory—air, land, sea, sub-sea, and space—from which to better operate and attack. Having positional advantage includes denying this territory and freedom of movement to the enemy. Attaining this advantage involves combat operations. [15]

---

[15] (1995, May). FM 100-7, chptr 3 Strategic and Operational-Level Perspective.

The key elements of theater and operational design reinforce the concepts of operational art and design consist of the—Objective, Sequence of operations and use of resources, Phases, Branches and sequels, Sequential and simultaneous warfare, and Logistics. The senior army commander's effective use of operational art and design elements translates theater strategy and the campaign into operational and, ultimately, tactical action. No specific level of command is concerned solely with operational art and design. The level of command that has the responsibility to link strategic aims with tactical execution varies in military operations. The theater commander and subordinate operational-level commanders may control large military formations over great geographic distances while sequencing tactical military operations in pursuit of strategic or operational objectives. Conversely, operational-level commanders may control relatively small military formations conducting specific, short-term operations for the same purpose. Senior army commanders practice operational art across the range of military operations. Whatever the environment (peacetime, conflict, or war), the operational-level commander links theater strategy and campaigns to tactical execution by effectively sequencing operations over time.

The objective is the central element of operational design because it establishes the condition necessary to achieve the strategic aim. While the CINC initially keys on national or alliance strategic objectives, he also supplements them with theater strategic and operational objectives. To ensure clarity of strategic and operational intent when conducting subordinate campaigns, JFCs may identify and carefully describe operational objectives from the CINC's specified and implied tasks.

The sequence of operations and use of resources are closely related elements of theater and operational design. The operational-level commander links theater strategy and campaigns to tactical execution by effectively sequencing major operations and battles over time. As described in FM 100-5, tempo and battle command contribute significantly to the effective sequencing of events. The JFC visualizes the sequence of operations necessary to achieve the desired conditions of the strategic end state. Without this linkage, operations are apt to become a series of disjointed events less likely to achieve the desired theater objectives. The visualization includes identifying the enemy center of gravity and culminating points and protecting the friendly center of gravity.

This process is useful when determining phases of a campaign, applying resources against these phases, and enabling the JFC to envision requirements for branches or sequels.

Generally, the campaign is divided into phases that focus on major changes in the nature of the total effort, such as defensive to offensive, decisive maritime action, and decisive continental action. Some campaigns are naturally progressive in their phasing (establish sea control, gain a lodgment, initiate a major continental campaign), while others are more complex. The latter may be the case when the opponent has initiated hostilities and the theater commander must transition from an initial defense, to seizure of the initiative, and eventually to offensive operations to achieve the strategic goal. The main effort is to attack the centers of gravity simultaneously throughout the depth of the battle space. Often that effort is phased. Each phase in the campaign should lay the groundwork for its successor until a final decisive effort can be joined. A phase may orient on a physical objective or on establishing a certain advantageous condition. The description of each phase should identify the strategic tasks to be accomplished, together with the ultimate purpose—the why—of the strategic tasks. The description should include a narrative of the theater commander's strategic concept of how and when these strategic tasks are to be accomplished. It should also include an estimate of force requirements, as, well as major supporting operations necessary for the effort. These concepts and force estimates should be continually refined up to the time the operation order implementing that phase is required. Prior to terminating the phase or meeting the necessary conditions for moving to the next phase, planning will have begun and the refinement process to facilitate the transition will continue. The phasing and sequencing of operations should not be slow or methodical. However, as soon as conditions permit, the JFC strives to overwhelm the enemy throughout the depth of the battle space. He conducts simultaneous attacks throughout the depth to paralyze the enemy and force an early capitulation.

Besides phases, the JFC visualizes requirements over the full range ofoperations for branches to preserve freedom of action. Branches are contingency plans for changing disposition, orientation, or direction of movement and for accepting or declining battle. Sequels are actions taken after an event or battle and are based on possible outcomes—victory, defeat, or stalemate.

Sequels, for example, might reflect a potential transition from the strategic defense to a counteroffensive, to a withdrawal, or to an occupation. The visualization of branches and sequels is not simply a thought process of events.

This visualization is a parallel planning process that provides the command a valuable resource—time.

In considering phasing, the JFC addresses the problem of deployment to ensure that forces arrive at times and places that support the campaign. Because of limited resources, geographic considerations, and our system for organizing the force, the US may go to war in sequential phases. At the strategic level, sequential actions include mobilization, deployment, and sustainment of the sequential employment of forces. Because the US is strategically insular, plans are driven to exterior lines of communications (LOCs), and, with limited resources, the campaign is phased to achieve strategic ends. At the operational-level, sequencing may be seen more in terms of employment. Additionally, sustainment is a critical consideration in sequencing campaigns. The campaign establishes requirements for the procurement and apportionment of national resources from CONUS-sustaining bases. Forward bases must be established, LOCs must be opened and maintained, intermediate bases of operations must be established to support new phases, and priorities for services and support must be established by phase.

Logistics considerations, then, become key to sequencing the campaign plan.

Notwithstanding the generally sequential nature of campaign phases, some phases are conducted simultaneously—particularly in depth. Deployment may continue well after employment begins. Sustainment is conducted throughout. Redeployment may begin during post-hostility operations. Defense and offense operations are always interrelated. Also, sequential operations may be conducted in a single operation, for example, the raid into Libya.[16]

The Army may act as a service component functional component, sub-unified command, or JTF subordinate to the JFC during the conduct of operational-level activities. The ASCC, or ARFOR commander, acting in one or more of these roles at the operational level, plans and conducts subordinate campaigns, major operations, and operations to attain theater strategic and/or operational objectives to support the joint force mission. The JFC translates strategic guidance to operational terms in the form of an OPLAN or operations order (OPORD). This OPLAN/OPORD includes a clear mission and specific tasks to which the traditional military decision-making cycle is applied. The JFC provides a clear definition of the conditions that constitute the strategic

---

[16] FM 100-7 chpter 3, Theater Strategic Operational-Level Perspective.

and military end states. The conditions for the end states must exist before planning and execution of military operations can be effective. The Army operational-level commander may translate these conditions into a single military objective or phased military objectives expressed in major operations that support joint campaigns. The Army commander participates in the joint concurrent (parallel) planning process to help the JFC translate strategic direction and aims into a clearly defined and achievable end state and objective. Usually, the more intense the conflict and the more predominant the military factors, the easier it is to translate strategic direction into operational-level objectives. When the nonmilitary elements of national power dominate, the full use of military capability may be limited. Joint Pub 3-0 states that adaptive planning provides a range of options encompassing all the elements of national power (diplomatic, economic, informational, and military). The selection of military operational-level objectives tends to be more complex in MOOTW.[17]

Political & Diplomatic strategy can take the form of legitimacy and Letter of Demarche. Our extraordinary diplomatic leverage to reshape existing security and economic structures and create new ones ultimately relies upon American power. Economic and military might, as well as the power of our ideals, also makes America's diplomats the first among equals and enables us to help create the conditions necessary for U.S. interests to thrive.[18] At the same time, there are unprecedented opportunities to make the nation safer and more prosperous. Military might is unparalleled. The United States now has a truly global economy linked by an instantaneous communications network, which offers increasing opportunities for American jobs and American investment. The community of democratic nations is growing, enhancing the

---

[17] FM 100-7 chpter 3, Theater Strategic Operational-Level Perspective.

[18] (1996). 1996 National Security Strategy. The White House.

prospects for political stability, peaceful conflict resolution and greater dignity and hope for the people of the world. The international community is beginning to act together to address pressing global environmental needs. Never has American leadership been more essential—to navigate the shoals of the world's new dangers and to its dynamic economy, its powerful ideals and, above all, its people. The United States can and must make the difference through its engagement; but its involvement must be carefully tailored to serve its interests and priorities.[19]

President Clinton also stressed in the 1996 National Security Strategy that during the past three years of his administration, diplomacy backed by American power had produced impressive results: When Iraq moved forces towards Kuwait, the United States reacted swiftly and dispatched additional, large-scale forces to the region under the authority of the United Nations—but we were prepared to act alone, if necessary. In Haiti, it was only when the Haitian military learned that the 82nd Airborne Division was en route that the United States achieved peacefully what it was prepared to do under fire. In Bosnia, the U.S. achieved a breakthrough when U.S. diplomatic leadership was married to appropriate military power. After the fall of Zepa and Srebrenica, the United States secured an agreement from our NATO allies to meet further assaults on the UN safe areas with a decisive military response. American pilots participated in the NATO bombing campaign following the shelling of a Sarajevo marketplace, demonstrating U.S. resolve and helping to bring the parties to the negotiating table. U.S. leadership then seized the opportunity for peace that these developments created: U.S. diplomats, along with our Contact Group partners, brokered a cease-fire and after intensive U.S.-led negotiations in Dayton, Ohio, a comprehensive peace agreement. U.S. forces worked as part of a larger

---

[19] (1996). 1996 National Security Strategy. The White House.

NATO force—joined by forces from members of NATO's Partnership for Peace—to help implement the military aspects of the agreement and create the conditions for peace to take hold. In Rwanda and Somalia, only the American military could have accomplished what it did in these humanitarian missions, saving hundreds of thousands of lives. However, over the longer run U.S. interests were served by turning these operations over to multilateral peacekeeping forces once the immediate humanitarian crisis was addressed. No outside force can create a stable and legitimate domestic order for another society—that work can only be accomplished by the society itself. National security strategy reflects both America's interests and values. The U.S. commitment to freedom, equality and human dignity continues to serve as a beacon of hope to peoples around the world. The vitality, creativity and diversity of American society are important sources of national strength in a global economy increasingly driven by information and ideas. U.S. prospects in this new era are promising. The specter of nuclear annihilation had dramatically receded. The historic events of the past three years—including the handshake between Israel and the PLO, the peace treaty between Israel and Jordan, the transformation of South Africa to a multiracial democracy headed by President Mandela and the peace agreement to end the war in Bosnia—suggested this era's possibilities for achieving security, prosperity and democracy.[20]

President Clinton further stated that U.S. leadership must stress preventive diplomacy—through such means as support for democracy, economic assistance, overseas military presence, interaction between U.S. and foreign militaries and involvement in multilateral negotiations in the Middle East and elsewhere—in order to help resolve problems, reduce tensions and defuse conflicts before they become crises. U.S.

---

[20] (1996). 1996 National Security Strategy. The Whtie House.

national security strategy draws upon a range of political, military and economic instruments, and focuses on the primary objectives that President Clinton has stressed throughout his Administration: Enhancing Security. Taking account of the realities of the new international era with its array of new threats, a military capability appropriately sized and postured to meet the diverse needs of our strategy, including the ability, in concert with regional allies, to win two nearly simultaneous major regional conflicts. The U.S. will continue to pursue a combination of diplomatic, economic strategy and defense efforts, including arms control agreements, to reduce the danger of nuclear, chemical, biological and conventional conflict and to promote stability.

Economic strategy can be based on internal economic stability and sanctions. Section 603 of the Goldwater-Nichols Defense Department Reorganization Act of 1986, elaborates a national security strategy that is tailored for this new era and builds upon America's unmatched strengths. Focusing on new threats and new opportunities, its central goals are:

> To enhance our society with military forces that are ready to fight with effective representation abroad.

> To bolster America's economic revitalization.

> To promote democracy abroad.

From 1993-1996, President Clinton's Administration worked diligently to pursue these goals. This national security strategy report presents the strategy that has guided this effort. It is premised on a belief that the line between our domestic and foreign policies is disappearing—that we must revitalize our economy if we are to sustain our military forces, foreign initiatives and global influence, and that we must engage actively abroad if we are to open foreign markets and create jobs for our people. The U.S.

believed that its goals of enhancing our security, bolstering our economic prosperity and promoting democracy are mutually supportive. Secure nations are more likely to support free trade and maintain democratic structures. Free market nations with growing economies and strong and open trade ties are more likely to feel secure and to work toward freedom. Democratic states are less likely to threaten American interests and more likely to cooperate with the United States to meet security threats and promote free trade and sustainable development. These goals are supported by ensuring America remains engaged in the world and by enlarging the community of secure, free market and democratic nations.

Economic strength gives us a position of advantage on almost every global issue. For instance, American efforts in South Africa and our negotiations with North Korea demonstrate how the imposition—or the threat—of economic sanctions helps the U.S. to achieve its objectives as part of its determined diplomacy. That determined diplomacy also is reflected in its consistent effort to engage in productive relations with China across a broad range of issues, including regional security, nonproliferation, human rights and trade. Americans seek a strategic relationship with China, advancing our own national interests in key areas. It is this steady approach—asserting America's core national security interests while keeping in mind longer-term goals—that is the hallmark of determined diplomacy.[21] Also, on the economic front, Administration policies have created nearly 7.5 million American jobs and established the foundation for the global economy of the 21st Century.

American jobs and established the foundation for the global economy of the 21st Century:

The President worked with the Congress on effective measures to reduce the federal budget deficit and restore economic growth. These measures

---

[21] (1996). 1996 National Security Strategy. The White House.

help increase our competitiveness and strengthen our position in negotiations with other nations. Two million of the 7.5 million new jobs created in the last three years are a result of our efforts to expand market access for American products overseas. These efforts have also lead to the creation of over 3 million new small businesses and the lowest combined rates of unemployment and inflation in 25 years. The federal budget deficit has dropped three years in a row, from $290 billion to $164 billion a year. The President secured approval of the North American Free Trade Agreement (NAFTA), which creates the world's largest free trade zone and has already created nearly 310,000 American jobs. The vote for NAFTA marked a decisive U.S. affirmation of its international engagement. Through NAFTA's environmental and labor side agreements, we are working actively to protect the rights of workers and to reduce air and water pollution that crosses national boundaries. When Mexico came under short-term financial pressures in December 1994, the United States took the lead in marshaling international support to assist the country in meeting this challenge. NAFTA helped to protect and increase U.S. exports to that country—and the jobs they support—during the financial crisis and the subsequent adjustment period. We have also begun negotiations with Chile to join NAFTA. The Administration stood at the forefront of a multilateral effort to achieve history's most extensive market-opening agreements in the GATT Uruguay-round negotiations on world trade. Working with a bipartisan coalition in the Congress, the President secured approval of this path-breaking agreement and the resulting World Trade Organization, which will add $150 billion annually to the U.S. economy once fully phased in and create hundreds of thousands of jobs. The President convened the first meeting of leaders of the Asia Pacific Economic Cooperation (APEC) forum and took steps to expand our ties with the economies of the Asia-Pacific region, the fastest growing area in the world. At their second forum, APEC leaders embraced the goal of free trade within the region by 2020, and at their third meeting in Osaka in 1995, they formulated a positive action plan to facilitate and measure progress toward achieving that goal. That past year, the U.S. successfully negotiated historic trade agreements with our Asian trading partners, including China, Japan and Korea, all of which promote substantial new access for American products and which will foster new attitudes of openness toward our exports.

The President hosted the Summit of the Americas in December 1994, a historic gathering where the 34 democratic nations of the hemisphere committed themselves to completing negotiations by 2005 on a regional free-trade agreement. In June 1995, the United States hosted the Denver Trade Ministerial and Commerce Forum to promote trade liberalization and business facilitation throughout the Western Hemisphere. At President Clinton's initiative, the G-7 Leaders put forth at the Halifax Economic Summit extensive proposals to prepare our international financial institutions for the 21st Century, including institutional reforms to prevent and respond to financial crises, to promote sustainable development and to support the Middle East peace process. At the December 1995 U.S.-European Union Summit in Madrid, the President announced the New Transatlantic Agenda, including a Transatlantic Marketplace that will deepen our cooperation on economic issues.[22]

The questions remained, Is the country able to provide its people with basic human needs (foodstuffs, clean water, shelter, free and universal basic education, basic health care) and a relative level of comfort (quality of life), while also meeting defense requirements? A diversified yet integrated economy with competent workers and managers in Agriculture: foodstuffs, raw materials Infrastructure: Transport and communication networks Light industries: handicrafts, processing, consumer products Mining, refining, metallurgy, and heavy machine industries Banking, insurance, and other service industries High-technology industries Trade: internal commerce; international trade.[23]

---

[22] (1996). 1996 National Security Strategy. The White House.
[23] Power, Elements of National Power, Power Politics.

Informational/technological strategy can be informational credibility, deception, and psychological operations. Military operations of the future will be predicated on information dominance. Emerging technology enables the rapid collection, processing, and dissemination of an increasing volume of highly accurate strategic, operational, and tactical information. Much of this information comes from reconnaissance, surveillance, and intelligence assets in air and space but the national and international information infrastructure are of benefit as well. Control of the information spectrum will be pivotal to the outcome of conflict in the twenty-first century. It will involve not only the preservation of our own access to such information but also the denying of access to our adversaries. "Global awareness" will soon take its place alongside "global reach" and "global power" in the Air Force's sense of purpose and direction. Often, it is difficult for individuals and companies to process and make sense of information that now appears in multiple channels at incredible speed. Communications experts are in the perfect position to capitalize on this overload and confusion. And that is what is meant by the "Dawn of the Communications Age." Value lies in the ability to organize, analyze, and deliver complex information. The Communications Age is defined not by the quantity of information accessed and relayed, but the quality of how it's managed. By organize – it means—what is most important? What is the priority? By analyze— what does it mean? By delivery—how should the information be communicated and to whom? [24]

Space. The armed forces are vitally dependent on space systems for information, communications, and operational support that ranges from targeting assistance to weather reporting. It is clear that space will figure even larger in defense programs and strategies of the future. The

---

[24] Drobis, David (2000, June). Address to Chinese Public Relations Association. www.votd.com/drobis.htm.

Air Force launches and operates more than ninety percent of all Department of Defense space assets . The Air Force has also been designated as the Department of Defense executive agent for multi-user space systems. Leadership in the developing arena of space is a heavy responsibility, but one which the Air Force is well-suited to meet. The increasing importance of the military space program is such that it must be accorded priority in research, development, and funding by the Department of Defense and by the nation. Leading requirements include routine, affordable, reliable access to space and better systems to detect and track theater ballistic missile launches.[25]

March 1995, President Clinton ordered a sweeping reexamination of the U.S. Governments approach to putting science and technology to the service of national security and global stability in light of the changed security environment, increasing global economic competition and growing budgetary pressures. The resulting National Security Science and Technology Strategy is the country's first comprehensive Presidential statement of national security science and technology priorities.[26]

In SOFTWAR, TV reporter Chuck de Caro describes in chilling detail how global television has been used to shape a nation's will, and how vulnerable and defenseless the U.S. is to this new form of information warfare. He describes exactly how the medium of television—which defines events by viewer perception of images and sound, rather than reality—has been used to influence public thinking and behavior. This essay explains how, by instantly creating domestic political pressures, an opponent could preclude our political leadership from acting, thus freezing the U.S. military and rendering policy and military capabilities

---

25 AFA 1996-97 Statement of Policy.
26 (1996). 1996 National Security Strategy. The White House.

ineffectual. "Hatred had to be created artificially [to fan the fires of pan-Serbiasm] and the key instrument was television." The author believes that the U.S. has ignored the use of TV to positively influence the course of human events around the globe.

Warfare in the Information Age Information Warfare: The Future is about the cooperation, rather than confrontation and "brute force," as an agent of change in the world of interconnected systems; and how, in the process, we can redefine our notions of security. John Petersen describes himself as a "futurist" and his essay portrays a world where systems must "cooperate" rather than "compete;" where the contest over information is not a "zero-sum" game; and, where our industrial-age experiences and tools will not be effective. It is a world where ideas, messages, and admonitions are focused on individuals and groups, who never figure out that they have been soldiers in a battle: unwitting "victims" of subliminal communications. He asks how one can plan for change when "everything is connected to everything else," and all systems are "out of control?" He says that the process of getting all of the parts of a complex system to work together requires communications—knowledge must be shared—with little concern over cultural or political boundaries. Information warfare is a revolutionary strategy that can strengthen our national security apparatus by enhancing the effectiveness of our military forces. But the rush to a new form of conflict is risky because it rests on new, poorly understood, controversial and unproved assumptions and strategies about our ability to dominate the information spectrum. Rush to Information-Based Warfare Gambles with National Security describes a quest for a strategy that is impeded by the lack of historical precedent, common definitions, doctrine, guiding principles, and a national-level policy to integrate and synchronize military initiatives with complementary actions of non-defense activities. This essay contrasts IW with "resource-based warfare"—a proven strategy that made minimal demands on national intellect or foresight, and was forgiving of an apathetic public and procrastinating political leaders—for one which depends on the agility and decisive firepower of a smaller force that has been empowered and effectively enlarged through superior knowledge. A Theory of Information Warfare (IW): Preparing for 2020, is about epistemological warfare and the moral and ethical risks of this form on conflict directed, not necessarily against military forces, but against the adversary's knowledge and belief systems. Richard Szafranski argues that the adversary is subdued by IW when he behaves in ways that are coincident with the ways in which we intend for him to behave. This essay describes IW at the operational and the strategic levels, and suggests that the Congress may conclude that employment at the operational level is useful and necessary, but employment against noncombatants, or their employment at the strategic level is wrong. The essay examines the ethical, moral and legal aspects of conflict that cannot discriminate between combatants and noncombatants, and where the interposition of a false reality ultimately may be wrongful and inhumane. Ethical Conundra of Information Warfare. With every grisly detail of our military activities covered by television, and viewed by the family over the dinner hour, the U.S. seeks tools and methods for a "clean war," and it has invented a host of "nonlethal" techniques, among which is Information Warfare. But, Winn Schwartau asks, is IW really non-lethal—disrupting a nations power, transportation and banking system, for example—if these might violate the political, social and ethical consciences of our own nation, as well as our friends. He believes the U.S. should face the ethical consequences of this form of conflict now, and announce to the world our intentions on how we will fight and defend ourselves in the Information Age. This essay presents several hypothetical scenarios for the employment of Information Warfare, and invites the reader to contemplate the ethical issues.

Coming to Terms With Information Warfare, by Alan Campen is an essay about the varying and often contradictory interpretations of the meaning, intent and weapons, targets, and tactics of Information Warfare. It also discusses the assumptions, uncertainties and risks to ourselves—as the most dependent of nations upon vulnerable information systems—if we employ some of these tools and methods in ways that have no doctrinal, ethical, legal, or moral precedents.

The varying terms are explained and the underlying assumptions of each tested for dependencies and vulnerabilities. The essay provides a simple test to determine the meaning and implications of the often-conflicting terminology, and provides conclusions and recommendations. While the public ponders the unsettling questions about vulnerabilities to the nation's information infrastructure, a little-known agency—born in response to earlier concerns about the health of the nations communications structure—has quietly moved to address the multiple challenges of deregulation of the telecommunications industry, and the nations growing dependence upon a vulnerable Public Network. Information Assurance: Implications to National Security and Emergency Preparedness, by James Kerr of the National Communications System staff, describes the work underway, in cooperation with industry, to assess this nations dependencies upon "information assurance," and the actions needed to deter, prevent, or mitigate attacks on the public network. This essay reports on the conclusions of several recent assessments of security weaknesses in the public network, and on changes in the FY1996 National Defense Authorization Act, calling for a national policy and an architecture for an indications and warning center to detect attacks on the National Information Infrastructure.[27] U.S. intelligence capabilities are critical instruments of our national power and integral to implementing our national security strategy. Strong intelligence

---

[27] Campen, Alan, Derth, D. H., & Goodden, Thomas R. (1996). CyberWar Security Strategy and conflict in. the Info Age.

capabilities are needed to protect our nation by providing warning of threats to U.S. national security, by providing support to the policy and military communities to prevail over these threats and by identifying opportunities for advancing our national interests through support to diplomacy. Decisionmakers, military commanders and policy analysts at all levels rely on the intelligence community to collect information unavailable from other sources and to provide strategic and tactical analysis to help surmount challenges to our national interests and security.

Because of the change in the security environment since the end of the Cold War, intelligence must address a wider range of threats and policy needs. In this demanding environment, the intelligence community must maintain its global reach, refine and further focus its collection efforts and work even more closely with the policy departments. Moreover, its analytic effort must provide a coherent framework to help senior U.S. officials manage a complex range of military, political and economic issues. Intelligence emphasis must be placed on preserving and enhancing those collection and analytic capabilities that provide unique information against those states and groups that pose the most serious threats to U.S. security. To build greater focus, direction and responsiveness into these intelligence activities, the President signed a Presidential Decision Directive (PDD) on intelligence priorities. This Directive established for the first time a series of categories of intelligence needs. This PDD is a flexible document designed to accommodate shifting priorities within the categories. Current Presidential priorities include:

Warning and management of threats that pose a direct or immediate threat to U.S. interests.

"Rogue states" whose policies are consistently hostile to the United States.

Countries that possess strategic nuclear forces that can pose a threat to the United States and its allies.

Command and control of nuclear weapons and control of nuclear fissile materials.

Transnational threats such as proliferation of weapons of mass destruction, international narcotics trafficking, international terrorism and international organized crime.

Ongoing or potential major regional conflicts where the United States has national security interests.

Intensified counterintelligence against hostile foreign intelligence services.

U.S. intelligence must not only monitor traditional threats but also assist the policy community to forestall new and emerging threats, especially those of a transnational nature. In carrying out these responsibilities, the intelligence community must:

Support U.S. military operations worldwide. Whenever U.S. forces are deployed, the highest priority is to ensure that our military commanders receive the timely information required to execute successfully their mission while minimizing the loss of American lives. Support diplomatic efforts in pursuit of U.S. foreign policy objectives by providing policymakers and diplomats timely intelligence on political developments in key areas such as the Middle East, the Balkans and North Korea. Provide worldwide capabilities to detect, identify and deter efforts of foreign nations to develop weapons of mass destruction and ancillary delivery systems. Gather information on terrorist activities aimed at U.S. persons or interests and help thwart such activities whether conducted by well-organized groups or loose associations of disaffected individuals intent on striking at the United States. Provide worldwide capabilities to gather timely intelligence on current and emerging information technologies or infrastructure that may potentially threaten U.S. interests at home or abroad. Contribute where appropriate to policy efforts aimed at bolstering our economic prosperity. Provide the timely information necessary to monitor treaties, promote democracy and free markets, forge alliances and track emerging threats. The collection and analysis of economic intelligence will play an increasingly important role in helping policymakers understand economic trends. Economic intelligence can help by identifying threats to private U.S. economic enterprises from foreign intelligence services as well as unfair trading practices. Intelligence must also identify emerging threats that could affect the international economy and the stability of some nation states, such as the upsurge in international organized crime and illegal trafficking in narcotics. The development and implementation of U.S. policies to promote democracy abroad relies on sound intelligence support. In order to forecast adequately dangers to democracy abroad, the intelligence community and policy departments must track political, economic, social and military developments in those parts of the world where U.S. interests are most heavily engaged and where collection of information from open sources is inadequate. This often leads to early warning of potential crises and facilitates preventive diplomacy. Improving the management of intelligence resources and focusing on the principal concerns of policymakers and military commanders enhances the value of intelligence and contributes to our national well-being. The establishment, for example, of the National Imagery and Mapping Agency will provide a more integrated imagery capability that will be especially important in providing warning of threats to U.S. and allied interests and in supporting crisis management and military operations. Intelligence producers must develop closer relationships with the users of intelligence to make products more responsive to current consumer needs. This includes identifying emerging threats to modern information systems and supporting the development of protection strategies. The continuous availability of intelligence, especially during crises, is of crucial importance. Also underlying all intelligence activities must be an increased awareness of, and enhanced capabilities in, counterintelligence. Finally, to enhance the study and support of worldwide environmental, humanitarian and disaster relief activities, technical intelligence assets—especially imagery—must be directed to a greater degree toward collection of data on these subjects.

The Information Age has come under the view of historians who are well-grounded in the agricultural and industrial revolutions, but who seem inattentive to the unique factors that are shaping the Information Revolution. Information

Age/Information War is an historical analysis of the information quotient in military and geopolitical affairs; an era of fundamental and global change in intellectual, philosophical, cultural and social terms. The Revolution in Military Affairs: The Information Dimension takes the reader on a sweeping overview of the military role today, and what it might be like under varying interpretations of information warfare. Michael Brown begins with the synergistic effects of information on military operations, describing an Information-based revolution that is producing a new environment from technologies that already exist, and from weapons that have either been built, or are on the drawing board. He examines the impact of creating a Smart Nation of information technologies on intelligence (where most targets will be discovered), on logistics (where "just in time" means no expensive and vulnerable baggage train), on command and control (where simulation replaces sand tables and where command arrangements combine hierarchical and non-hierarchical processes); and, where "fire support" becomes precision strike.

Creating a Smart Nation: Information Strategy, Virtual Intelligence, and Information Warfare is a sweeping indictment of our national security posture.

Robert Steele asserts that national security is at risk by confronting current threats with 19th century concepts; for preoccupation with digital technology; and by an intelligence community optimized, less for thoughtful analysis than for "the collecting of secrets." This essay examines structural and policy defects in the processes of intelligence, and calls for a National Information

Strategy built upon political, military, economic and cultural objectives, to guide preparation for conflict in the Information Age. The Role of The Media is about a new reality where the media believes that it has not only a duty to report the news, but also has the power to influence events. We live and work in a physical world where safety and well-being heavily depend upon the ability to fix people, things and transactions precisely and accurately in place and in time. Cyberspace knows no such boundaries and the potential for fraud, abuse, misuse in this virtual world are significant when jurisdictions cannot be determined. Grounding Cyberspace in the Physical World is about the use of the Global Positioning System to aid personal and network security by affixing a secure, precise and continuous location signature to all terminals, fixed or mobile. Professor George Stein writes about a new strategic level of warfare made possible by new technologies and their use to manipulate reality, rather than simply multiplying the power of conventional armed forces in combat. This essay describes the potential for altering reality with a "fictive" universe of altered data: replacing the opponents "known" universe with an "alternative reality." This essay is about defining and developing a strategy for information warfare, against new and dangerous non-state players in cyberspace who can wage attacks on a global basis. Strategic Information Warfare and Comprehensive Situational Awareness also questions the wisdom and utility of the JCS decision to adopt C2W as the military component of information warfare. Professor Daniel Kuehl contends that information warfare must reach out to encompass national-level political, economic, military and social systems—including diplomatic and economic actions—by destructive or non-lethal military operations. He argues that the narrow definition precludes discussion of the legal, political and interagency issues that are a part of a strategic perspective.

Military strategy can be based on military flexible deterrent options and strike options. In a statement during the 2000 debates, Vice President Gore Stated "Right now our military is the strongest in the entire history of the world. I will—I pledge to you I will do whatever is necessary to make sure that it stays that way."[28] US Armed Forces help shape the international environment through deterrence, peacetime engagement activities, and active participation and leadership in alliances. Critical to deterrence are our conventional warfighting capabilities and our nuclear forces. Deterrence rests on a potential adversary's perception of our capabilities and commitment, which are demonstrated by our ability to bring decisive military power to bear and by communication of US intentions. Engagement activities, including information sharing and contacts between our military and the armed forces of other nations, promote trust and confidence and encourage measures that increase our security and that of our allies, partners, and friends. By increasing understanding and reducing uncertainty, engagement builds constructive security relationships, helps to promote the development of democratic institutions, and helps keep some countries from becoming adversaries tomorrow. Responding to the Full Spectrum of Crises. The US military will be called upon to respond to crises across the full range of military operations, from

---

[28] Debate Transcripts 2000 17 Oct.

humanitarian assistance to fighting and winning major theater wars (MTW), and conducting concurrent smaller scale contingencies. Our demonstrated ability to rapidly respond and to decisively resolve crises provides the most effective deterrent and sets the stage for future operations if force must be used. Should deterrence fail, it is imperative that the United States be able to defeat aggression of any kind. Especially important is the ability to deter or defeat nearly simultaneous large scale, cross border aggression in two distant theaters in overlapping time frames, preferably in concert with allies. The ability to rapidly defeat initial enemy advances short of their objectives in two theaters in close succession reassures our allies and ensures the protection of our worldwide interests. America must also be prepared to conduct several smaller-scale contingency operations at the same time, as situations may dictate the employment of US military capabilities when rapid action is required to stabilize a situation. Preparing Now for an Uncertain Future. As we move into the next century, it is imperative that the United States maintain the military superiority essential to our global leadership. Our strategy calls for transformation of our doctrine and organizations and a stabilized investment program in robust modernization that exploits the Revolutions in Military Affairs (RMA) and Business Affairs (RBA).

The National Military Strategy describes four strategic concepts that govern the use of our forces to meet the demands of the strategic environment. Strategic Agility is the timely concentration, employment and sustainment of US military power anywhere, at our own initiative, and at a speed and tempo that our adversaries cannot match. It is an important hedge against the uncertainty we face. It allows us to conduct multiple missions, across the full range of military operations, in geographically separated regions of the world. Overseas presence is the visible posture of US forces and infrastructure strategically positioned forward, in and near key regions. Forces present overseas promote stability, help prevent conflict, and ensure the protection of US interests. Our overseas presence demonstrates our determination to defend US, allied, and friendly interests while ensuring our ability to rapidly concentrate combat power in the event of crisis. Power Projection is the ability to rapidly and effectively deploy and sustain US military power in and from multiple, dispersed locations until conflict resolution. Power projection provides the flexibility to respond swiftly to crises, with force packages that can be adapted rapidly to the environment in which they must operate, and if necessary, fight their way into a denied theater. Decisive Force is the commitment of sufficient military power to overwhelm an adversary, establish new military conditions, and achieve a political resolution favorable to US national interests. Together, these four strategic concepts emphasize that America's military must be able to employ the right mix of forces and capabilities to provide the decisive advantage in any operation.

America's Armed Forces are the preeminent military force in the world, persuasive in peace and decisive in war. To successfully implement the strategy of shaping, responding, and preparing, the forces and capabilities recommended in the QDR report are essential. Equally critical to the success of strategy are the men and women who comprise our military forces. The Services must continue to recruit, train, and maintain a high quality force to ensure our nation's security. Forces must maintain the high state of readiness that is essential to global leadership; thus the means by which we achieve, maintain, and evaluate our readiness demand continued emphasis. Our military must be ready to fight as a coherent joint force fully interoperable and seamlessly integrated. Capitalizing on technology will also be central to maintaining military superiority. Our modernization effort will focus on those technologies that improve the combat effectiveness of our Armed Forces while enhancing the interoperability and integration of the Total Force. Modernization is not an end in itself, but a means to improve the capabilities of our warfighters across the full range of military operations from peacetime engagement activities to war. [29] A year-long assessment of the strategic environment was completed that underscored the continuing importance of robust American military power. While the U.S. no longer face the threat of a rival superpower, there are states and other actors who can challenge us and our allies conventionally and by asymmetric means such as terrorism and weapons of mass destruction. The rise of regional powers is leading to a multi-polar world that can be either more secure or more dangerous—hence the importance of the President's "imperative of engagement" described herein. The military has an important role in engagement—helping to shape the international environment in appropriate ways to bring about a more peaceful and stable world. The purpose of our Armed Forces, however, is to deter and defeat threats of organized violence to our country and its interests. While fighting and winning two nearly simultaneous wars remains the foremost task, but is changing, we must also respond to a wide variety of other potential crises. As we take on these diverse missions, it is important to emphasize the Armed Forces' core competence: we fight. That must be the primary consideration in the development and employment of forces.[30] The Armed Forces are the Nation's military instrument for ensuring our security. Accordingly, the primary purpose of US Armed Forces is to deter threats of organized violence against the United States and its interests, and to defeat such threats should deterrence fail. The military is a complementary element of national power that stands with the other instruments wielded by our government. The Armed Forces core competence is the ability to apply decisive military power to deter or defeat aggression and achieve our national security objectives.

---

[29] (1997). Executive Summary Strategy. www.dtic.miljcs/nms/executiv.htm.

[30] (1996). National Military Strategy. The White House.

Our Armed Forces foremost task is to fight and win our Nation's wars. Consequently, America's Armed Forces are organized, trained, equipped, maintained, and deployed primarily to ensure that our Nation is able to defeat aggression against our country and to protect our national interests.

US national interests fall into three categories. First in priority are our vital interests; those of broad, overriding importance to the survival, security, and territorial integrity of the United States. At the direction of the NCA, the Armed Forces are prepared to use decisive and overwhelming force, unilaterally if necessary, to defend America's vital interests. Second are important interests; those that do not affect our national survival but do affect our national well-being and the character of the world in which we live.

The use of our Armed Forces may be appropriate to protect those interests. Third, armed forces can also assist with the pursuit of humanitarian interests when conditions exist that compel our nation to act because our values demand US involvement. In all cases, the commitment of US forces must be based on the importance of the US interests involved, the potential risks to American troops, and the appropriateness of the military mission.

Throughout our history, America's Armed Forces have responded to a variety of national needs other than waging wars. The security environment we face includes threats to our country and to our interests that are not "war" in the classical sense, and yet may call for military forces. Terrorism, weapons of mass destruction (WMD), illegal drug-trafficking , and other threats at home or abroad may exceed the capacity of other agencies and require the use of military forces, depending upon applicable law, the direction of the NCA, and the national interest involved. In addition, military resources will continue to support civil authorities in executing missions such as civil works, disaster relief, and domestic crises.

The President's National Security Strategy for a New Century stresses "the imperative of engagement" and enhancing our security through integrated approaches that allow the Nation to Shape the international environment; Respond to the full spectrum of crises; and prepare now for an uncertain future. The U.S. strategic approach uses all appropriate instruments of national power to influence the actions of other states and non-state actors, exert global leadership, and remain the preferred security partner for the community of states that share our interests. The Armed Forces play a key role in this effort. The United States unparalleled military capabilities form the foundation of mutually beneficial alliances and security partnerships, undergird stability in key regions, and buttress the current worldwide climate of confidence that encourages peace, economic growth, and democratization. Our global engagement makes the world safer for our Nation, our citizens, our interests, and our values.[31]

But military force remains an indispensable element of our nation's power. Our nation must maintain military forces sufficient to deter diverse threats and, when necessary, to fight and win against our adversaries. While many factors ultimately contribute to our nation's safety and well-being, no single component is more important than the men and women who wear America's uniform and stand sentry over our security. Their skill, service and dedication constitute the core of our defenses. Today our military is the best-equipped, best-trained and best-prepared fighting force in the world. Time after time in the last three years, our troops demonstrated their continued readiness and strength: moving with lightning speed to head off another Iraqi threat to Kuwait;

---

31 (1997). Executive Summary Strategy. www.dtic.miljcs/nms/executive.htm.

helping to save hundreds of thousands of lives in Rwanda; giving freedom and democracy back to the people of Haiti; and helping enforce UN mandates in the former Yugoslavia and subsequently deploying forces under NATO command to help implement the peace agreement in Bosnia. I am committed to ensuring that this military capability is not compromised. U.S. military forces are critical to the success of our strategy. This nation has unparalleled military capabilities: the United States is the only nation able to conduct large-scale and effective military operations far beyond its borders. This fact, coupled with our unique position as the security partner of choice in many regions, provides a foundation for regional stability through mutually beneficial security partnerships. Our willingness and ability to play a leading role in defending common interests also help ensure that the United States will remain an influential voice in international affairs—political, military and economic—that affect our well-being, so long as we retain the military wherewithal to underwrite our commitments credibly. To protect and advance U.S. interests in the face of the dangers and opportunities outlined earlier, the United States must deploy robust and flexible military forces that can accomplish a variety of tasks:

Deterring and Defeating Aggression in Major Regional Conflicts. Our forces must be able to help offset the military power of regional states with interests opposed to those of the United States and its allies. To do this, we must be able to credibly deter and defeat aggression by projecting and sustaining U.S. power in more than one region if necessary. Providing a Credible Overseas Presence. U.S. forces must also be forward deployed or stationed in key overseas regions in peacetime to deter aggression and advance U.S. strategic interests. Such overseas presence demonstrates our commitment to allies and friends, underwrites regional stability, ensures familiarity with overseas operating environments, promotes combined training among the forces of friendly countries and provides timely initial response capabilities.

The Bush administration is shifting the direction of US strategic thinking. Priority will be given to the technological race and to the development and deployment of flexible, hi-tech forces capable of intervening anywhere in the world, to ensure the lasting primacy of US armed forces. [32]

---

[32] America's Military Revolution.

Chapter 2

What Leading Experts of Military Strategy Say About Center of Gravity

Joint Publication 3-0 says, "at the strategic level, center of gravity might include…an alliance, national will, or public support". Joint Level says that the center of gravity are those characteristics, capabilities, or locations from which a military derives its freedom of action, physical strength, or will to fight. The United States Army says that center of gravity is that characteristic, capability, or location from which a military force derives its freedom of action, physical strength, or will to fight. The United States Navy says that center of gravity is that characteristic from which enemy and friendly forces derive their freedom of action, physical strength, or will to fight. The United States Marines say that Strategic Center of Gravity is that objective whose seizure, destruction, or neutralization will have a profound impact on enemy leadership's will or ability to continue the struggle. Operational Center of

Gravity is that concentration of the enemy's military power that is most dangerous to us or stands between us and the accomplishment of our strategic mission. The United States Air Force definition of center of gravity is the same as the Joint definition. There is an absence of a universally accepted Joint Theory of Center of Gravity. There must be a move to develop one theory and use that theory to analyze terrorism, determining its decision points and vulnerabilities in order to solve the current crisis. A review of leading authorities shows how they view center of gravity. Starting with Clausewitz, he felt that center of gravity at the operational level is the concentration of combat power. He felt that at every level of war there is a different center of gravity. Strategic examples according to Clausewitz are a nation's capital, a city, its leaders or even public opinion. COL Wells felt that a center of gravity is the relevant mass of a combatant's combat power that is made significant by his corresponding will to use it. Mendal feels that the center of gravity is the derivative of the aims or objectives established at the level you are planning. Mendal thinks that not all sources of strength are center of gravities. Selecting a center of gravity brings clarity of purpose to the process of strategic planning. The center of gravity links strategic aims and the employment of forces. Izzo points out that the center of gravity is not an enemy weakness. There is no easy approach in identifying the center of gravity. He feels that by agreeing on the center of gravity, it will focus the specific command. Among these experts and Services there are multiple theories and definitions as to what comprises center of gravity. These varying opinions must be weighed and measured and brought to some common denominator in order to effectively apply the concept to solving a nation's problems. This must be done to solve the problem on how to combat terrorism. This must be done to identify the underpinning that will allow it to be defeated.

Each of the experts gives guidance in determining center of gravities. Clausewitz says that every level of war has a different center of gravity.

One must determine the center of gravity first at each level. He says that one can find the enemy center of gravity where the concentration of combat power is, it is always found where the mass is concentrated most densely. It is vital to accomplish his aims. COL Wells guidance is that we must move away from doctrinal frameworks of center of gravity when we consider Operations Other Than War scenarios (Somalia and Terrorism) and probe into the theoretical basis of center of gravities. Mendal's guidance is that center of gravity is the derivative of the aims or objectives established at the level you are planning. He feels that one must submit each potential center of gravity to a validity test. If one desires to impose his will upon a center of gravity, will that action create a cascading deteriorating effect on morale, cohesion and will to fight that prevents the enemy from achieving his aims and allows the achievement of our own? If I have a valid center of gravity, do I have a feasible ability to impose my will over it? If I cannot, or not completely, consider another potential center of gravity. Mendal says that center of gravities are dynamic and may change as the conflict evolves (appropriate to the political aim and nature of the conflict). He says that the strategic level is dominant in the continuum of war because it is at this level that the political, economic, military and other aims are defined and thus the importance of planning from the top down. Izzo states that the enemy's aims must be determined. The aim and the combat power allocated to achieve that aim is intimately linked. His center of gravity is the essence of his combat power enabling him to achieve that goal. D'Amura's guidance is that discerning enemy intent is very useful in identifying the center of gravity.

Do any of the experts make a distinction between strategic and operational centers of gravity? Clausewitz and Mendel are the only two who do make distinctions. Clausewitz says that every level of war has a different center of gravity. It can be found where the concentration of combat power is; it is always found where the mass is concentrated most densely. It is vital to accomplish his aims. Center of gravity at the operational level is the concentration of combat power of the enemy forces. Mendal says that the strategic center of gravity serves as the link between strategic aims and the operational employment of forces by the commander in charge.

The above discussion and points of views were observed being debated by senior officers of the Third U.S. Army, now deployed to Kuwait as part of Operation Enduring Freedom and responsible for all land operations for the campaign. Each article was discussed for its impact on changes to doctrine and how to identify centers of gravity. The group came to the conclusion after several meetings with the Commanding General that a joint definition needed to drive the Services to understanding center of gravity. It would therefore make accepting the change in doctrine easier and quicker.

Still others feel that center of gravity is not relevant as cited by various campaigns that follow: An important element of emerging joint doctrine is the idea that potential enemies have centers of gravity and critical vulnerabilities. Joint Publication 3-0, Doctrine for Joint Operations, states, "The essence of operational art lies in being able to mass effects against the enemy's sources of power in order to destroy or neutralize them. In theory, destruction or neutralization of enemy centers of gravity is the most direct path to victory." Navy and Marine Corps doctrine echo this focus. Both Naval Doctrine Publication-1, Naval Warfare, and Marine Corps Doctrine Publication-1, Warfighting, talk of concentrating effort on enemy centers of gravity to win decisively. The imagery is powerful and has strong appeal:

> It is campaign winning.
>
> It avoids heavy casualties.
>
> It has deep roots in Army and Air Force doctrine.
>
> It gives intellectual focus to planning.

Unfortunately, it often is a mirage. These concepts may be good in theory, but they rarely exist in the real world in a way useful for military planners. The problem is not, as some authors suggest, that centers of gravity are hard to identify and therefore underused by planners; the problem is that centers of gravity and critical vulnerabilities just are not there. In addition, their pursuit often overpromises what a campaign can achieve and can distract from more limited, but achievable, objectives. To illustrate this, suppose we could go back to the Tarawa battle of 1943, and armed with all our postwar research and analysis, could advise Major General H. M. Smith about the battle ahead. What would we tell him? Certainly we would tell him about the reef (too shallow on the lagoon side). We would tell him that prelanding bombardments need to be much longer than he believes. We would remind him not to reinforce failure in landing his reserve but to take advantage of success. But there is nothing useful we could say about critical enemy vulnerabilities or centers of gravity. Japanese capabilities had to be destroyed piece by piece. There was no point so vulnerable that its destruction would produce the collapse of resistance. Communications? Leadership? Supplies? In the actual event, the United States destroyed all of these elements, but fierce resistance still continued. Many U.S. actions produced battlefield advantage—pre-invasion bombardment, isolation of the garrison, decentralized tactical leadership—but there was nothing that could be termed a critical enemy vulnerability. Before going any further, it probably is worth reviewing the existing definitions of these terms:

Centers of gravity: "Those characteristics, capabilities, or localities from which a military force derives its freedom of action, physical strength, or will to fight". [33]

---

[33] Joint Publication 1-02, DoD Dictionary of Military and Associated Terms.

Critical vulnerabilities: Enemy weaknesses that, when attacked and destroyed or neutralized, produce decisive results, disproportional to the military resources applied.

Chapter 3

How the Center of Gravity was applied to the Gulf War, Panama Invasion, Somalia Operation, and is being applied to our current war on terrorism

The Gulf War

These definitions can be subjected to considerable analysis, commentary, and refinement. Dr. Joseph Strange of the Marine Corps War College has written an entire monograph on these and related terms, pointing out inconsistencies among the services and proposing doctrinal modifications. The purpose here, however, is to explore the broader usefulness of the terms. Let's look at another example: Desert Storm, the current model for a joint campaign. From a planning perspective, one observes that the Army, Navy, and Air Force each aimed their component campaigns at what they believed to be the critical Iraqi vulnerability and center of gravity: The Air Force devoted considerable effort to attacking strategic targets—electrical production, telecommunications, military production, oil refining—that could have effects only in the long term, far beyond the intended coalition campaign. By attacking these infrastructure targets, however, the air planners hoped to inflict such pain that the Iraqi leaders would opt to change their policies. The Army's planning focused on the Republican Guard, Generals Norman Schwarzkopf and Colin Powell believing that these divisions were the glue that held together Saddam's regime. Without the Republican Guard, they reasoned, Saddam would not be able to suppress dissent and would fall from power. (Originally, the Air Force planners had not even targeted the Republican Guard, which they regarded as a tactical distraction.) The Navy, in addition to its participation in the air war, conducted a traditional maritime blockade, aimed at strangling commerce and interdicting the export of Iraq's primary economic resource, oil. Arguably, all these efforts had some success. The strategic attacks on Iraqi infrastructure severely disrupted their economy. The Army's attack on the Republican Guard (combined with the air attacks) cut the Guard's strength in half The naval campaign completely cut off trade, especially the vital oil exports—and does so to this day . Nevertheless, all failed in their ultimate objective, to change the nature of the regime. Nothing we did forced Saddam out of power or made him change his basic attitudes. As a result, he continues to threaten his neighbors and to pursue weapons of mass destruction. The primary issue here is whether the concepts of critical vulnerabilities and centers of gravity have usefulness to planners. If they are to have any utility, they must do three things: They must offer the prospect of a disproportional effect—that friendly efforts concentrated on the selected enemy point will produce decisive results. They must not be obvious applications of traditional military theory. We do not need a new concept to tell us that turning an enemy's flank or cutting off his supplies will offer an important battle-field advantage. We know that already.

They must be executed at a practical level of effort. Any weakness can become "critical" if enough effort is brought to bear. It is not very helpful for planners to be told, "If you bomb the enemy intensively for extended periods, their morale will begin to crack." That is true for any army and is not a useful insight. The fundamental problem is that few situations in the real world meet these requirements. One finds many examples of vulnerabilities and campaign-winning tactics, but these display long-standing battlefield phenomenon—demoralization after protracted failure, collapse after being surrounded, disorganization after prolonged pounding by firepower. A few, quick examples make the point:

Discovering the reason for this resilience in military, political, and economic affairs is worthy of an article in its own right; however, one may infer from the few examples here and a review of history that the reason is related to two notions: (1) that human affairs are networks with many alternative paths, and (2) that enemies are dynamic actors, every bit as clever individually as we are, actively trying to thwart our designs. Army and Air Force doctrine regard networks as vulnerabilities—knock out one node and the whole network may collapse. The problem is that networks, by definition, have many paths leading to the same end. So it is with military activities. If a bridge at point A is destroyed, then the enemy will use the bridge at B, or the ford at C, or the ferry at D, or repair the bridge. As a result, doctrines that rely on precision effects against nodes of a network are on shaky ground. Instead of collapse, one sees instead coping mechanisms such as alternative routing, imaginative work arounds, and strict prioritization of flow traffic. Indeed, for these reasons, networks often are strengths, not weaknesses.

If this idea of centers of gravity and critical vulnerabilities does not come from history, where does it come from? This is clear. For the Army, the idea comes from Clausewitz. For the Air Force, it comes from a long line of air power proponents. For the Navy, interestingly, there is no equivalent; it has, in contrast, a doctrinal base emphasizing gradual effects over time. The U.S. Army always has studied Clausewitz. In the late 1980s, however, as it was revitalizing itself from the effects of Vietnam and the hollowness of the 1970s, the Army rediscovered his theories as part of its reemphasis on operational art. Following this increasing interest in Clausewitz has been an interest in centers of gravity, which Army doctrine describes as follows:

The concept of centers of gravity is key to all operational design. As with any complex organism, some components are more vital than others to the smooth and reliable operation of the whole. If these are damaged or destroyed, their loss unbalances the entire structure, producing a cascading deterioration of cohesion and effectiveness which may result in complete failure. Not surprisingly, then, Army doctrine states that "destruction, dislocation, or neutralization of the enemy center of gravity should prove decisive." This concept is applied at all levels, from the strategic to the tactical. It is easy, therefore, to see how the Army focused on the Republican Guard during Desert Storm. Its doctrine clearly implied that a center of gravity would exist and that the campaign plan should focus on it.

This interpretation of centers of gravity goes beyond Clausewitz, however. Clausewitz discusses centers of gravity at a very high level and in the context of a decisive battle: "Centers of gravity will be found wherever forces are most concentrated....It presents the most effective target for a blow." He calls identification of the centers of gravity a "major act of strategic judgment.? This is consistent with his focus on decisive battle as the means of decision in war, but there is nothing in Clausewitz like the Army's "network" theory. Air power, almost from its inception, has looked for decisive results from strategic effects against enemy centers of gravity and critical vulnerabilities. The prospect of "jumping over the trenches" to strike directly at an enemy's critical vulnerabilities has been extremely attractive. In its earliest form this strike was conceived as terror bombing against a vulnerable and easily demoralized civilian population.

Later it took the form of strikes against critical economic targets. In addition to theoretical reasons for such an approach there probably were institutional reasons—air forces needed a compelling rationale to make a place for themselves in a military structure dominated by older technologies and to justify the high costs of developing aviation technologies. Recently, air power theorist Colonel John Warden, U.S. Air Force (retired), has updated these theories and widely disseminated them. He states bluntly that "in all cases the enemy centers of gravity must be identified and struck." These centers of gravity he identifies as command-and-control capabilities and critical infrastructure. Nor is this just an Air Force theory now. Joint Publication 3-0 talks about air power "directly attacking strategic centers of gravity." Naval theory traditionally has had a very different orientation, arising from the inescapable fact that human beings live on land. It is therefore difficult, though perhaps not impossible, for naval forces to have effects that are both decisive and rapid. Far more common are the gradual processes of blockade and of wearing down enemy capabilities by attacks on the periphery. Although he envisioned the clash of mighty battle fleets, this was a means to an end, not the end itself. As a result, in traditional naval theory, the concept of striking at a center of gravity or a critical vulnerability is not strong or, for the most part, even evident. For this reason, Naval Doctrine Publication-1, Naval Warfare, seems to be an uncomfortable melding of traditional naval theory—with its focus on forward presence, deterrence, and sea control—and the newer, joint theories of centers of gravity, direct attack, and quick decisions, the whole overlaid with a discussion of land-oriented maneuver warfare. This may explain why its discussion of centers of gravity is so confusing, arguing, alone among the services, that there can be only a single center of gravity. Does it really matter that joint planning focuses on a questionable goal? Of course it does. When joint doctrine holds this concept up as the pinnacle of military objectives, planners will be encouraged to assume that critical vulnerabilities always exist and will look for them. Where such vulnerabilities are not evident, they will manufacture them. By looking for a silver bullet, our planners may ignore other, more modest but more realistic, objectives, or may oversell their plans as being potentially more effective than is the case. Arguably, this is what happened in Desert Storm, where we flawlessly executed plans aimed at critical vulnerabilities and centers of gravity, yet still had no decisive outcome. This last caution is particularly relevant in the current political-military environment. If military commanders tell civilian leaders (few of whom today have any military experience) that a campaign will attack critical enemy vulnerabilities and centers of gravity, then these leaders naturally will assume that the campaign will be shorter, less costly, and less risky than is often the case. Qualifying statements by the military cannot overturn these impressions, particularly since this is what civilians will want to believe. The national military strategy and Joint Vision 2010, which talk about achieving "full-spectrum dominance," encourage this belief in short, bloodless conflicts with accurately foreseeable courses of events. This belief is further encouraged by an abiding American faith in technological superiority and its battlefield advantages. This environment is a particular problem for naval planners. They are, arguably, being forced into an Army and Air Force doctrinal approach that does not fit naval capabilities well.

The foregoing discussion should not discourage planners from striving for victory or foster a belief that one approach is as good as another. It should not encourage any notion that broadly based attrition strategies are as good as focused, targeted strategies. High-priority targets still exist; some tactical approaches will produce better results than others; attacking weakness still is better than attacking strength. Nor is the point to eliminate any notion of critical vulnerabilities or centers of gravity because, occasionally, there may be a critical vulnerability that our forces can actually get at In retrospect, for instance, it seems that Saddam himself was a critical vulnerability, probably the only one. If he had been eliminated (and we tried), Iraqi policy might have changed. Nevertheless, a more useful focus for thinking about joint campaigns is needed, and the pieces are in place:

Joint Publication 1, Joint Warfare, talks about "sequenced and synchronized employment of all available land, sea, air, special operations, and space forces." Joint Publication 5-0, Doctrine for Planning Joint Operations, echoes this by describing campaign plans as "a series of joint major operations arranged in time, space, and purpose to achieve a strategic objective."

Naval Doctrine Publication-1 has a quite sensible discussion of how critical vulnerabilities may, or may not, exist and may, or may not, be accessible.

Marine Corps Doctrine Publication-1 talks of exploiting opportunities to create more opportunities that will, in the end, produce decisive results.

The common thread here is that, instead of focusing operations on a single decisive point by a single service, planners should focus on the more general goal of attaining battlefield advantage. Each advantage leads to another and another, the final result being decisive. The Falklands Campaign is a good model, where each effort—land, sea, and air—set up the next, until the final victory. In addition, this vision is more compatible with emerging notions of a joint campaign. Instead of each service trying on its own to land the decisive blow, the blows work together, building on each other, the result being decisive in a way that no single effort could be. Finally, this approach does not promise or imply more than it can deliver. It is less likely to lull civilian decision makers into a false sense of security because it implies that campaigns might be long and that the unexpected might occur. Joint doctrine today talks of focusing on critical vulnerabilities and centers of gravity to attain the desired end state of a joint campaign. Because critical vulnerabilities and centers of gravity so rarely exist, at least in a way useful for planners, joint doctrine would be better off focusing instead on battlefield advantages. The ultimate result would be the same—attaining the joint campaign's desired end state. The means, however, would focus on sequenced actions in a joint campaign, rather than on single-service attempts to land a decisive blow. Colonel Cancian, a reserve infantry officer, has served in a variety of billets from company to Marine expeditionary force level. He also has served at Headquarters Marine Corps and the Marine Corps Combat Development Command, where he worked extensively on joint issues. In civilian life, he works in the Office of the Secretary of Defense.[34]

Underlying the center of gravity are decision points. Key to attacking center of gravity is identifying these critical decisive points. FM 100-5 says that a decisive point provides commanders with a marked advantage over the enemy and is often geographical in nature. They could include elements that sustain such as a command post, critical boundary, airspace or communications node. Decision points are the keys to getting at the center of gravity. Wells says that planning and execution involves attacking various decisive points (using an indirect approach) and/or center of gravity (using a direct approach). An indirect approach

---

[34] Cancian, Mark COL (2001). U_S_ Naval Institute—Preceedings, Center of Gravity are a myth.

would be attacking the enemy's command and control, lines of communications, defensive capability, and then his primary center of gravity.

Panama

An analysis of the concept of centers of gravity can be depicted by examining Operation Just Cause, operations against Panama in 1988. Manuel Noriega, the head of the Panama Defense Forces (PDF), were serious threat to stability in the Western Hemisphere and to economics due to the necessity of the Panama Canal. The U.S. military invaded Panama with overwhelming forces and attacked numerous military targets across Panama. Lieutenant General Car Stiner, USA, who head the operation, had knowledge of the enemy that suggested the PDF was a centralized force with vulnerable centers of gravity incapable of numerous actions at once without direction from Noriega himself. Gen. Maxwell Thurman, designated Commander of US Southern Command, made suggestions to Stiner on the size of the forces to be involved in the invasion. He insisted that sufficient forces be involved in the invasion. Thurman believed that massing superior forces would save lives and lead to a quick success. Gen. Colin Powell, then Chairman of the Joint Chiefs of Staff, reviewed the plan and emphasized surprise, speed, and night operations during Operation Just Cause. The plan used maximum combat forces using minimum force. It was a complex plan involving Special Operation Forces and conventional forces carefully synchronized for maximum disruptive effect. Stiner's plan was for swift, violent, multiple forcible entry operations coupled with the employment of forces previously built up in-country, rather than for a drawn-out, piecemeal operation. By using in-country bases, Stiner ensured powerful operational reach. Using in-country bases made operational security a major concern for General Stiner. Equipment was moved under cover of darkness and concealed. PDF intelligence failures contributed significantly to US success in Operation JUST

CAUSE. Spanish-speakers on repeated tours with the in-country Army and Marine units contributed greatly to the success of this operation as well. The attack was made with simultaneity and depth by neutralizing, isolating, or protecting twenty-seven major targets in the operational area. Major target areas included Panama City, Rio Hato, and the Torrijos Airport. Stiner was able to prevent the PDF from taking large numbers of hostages or seizing the initiative even briefly. The rapid, overwhelming use of force shortened the invasion and reduced the loss of life. The PDF was not able to respond to multiple attacks. The entire task force was able to focus on accomplishment of assigned objectives and directed their major combat efforts towards the PDF's center of gravity form the outset of the operation to its speedy conclusion. General Stiner's concept allowed the sequencing of forces to take advantage of land, naval, air, and special operations forces in concentrating combat power. The Joint Special Operations Forces (SOF) helped to prepare the battlefield and then reinforced the main effort once the airborne attack was over.

The initial efforts to overwhelm the PDF was conducted by the US SOF conducting attacks across the country. They attacked PDF strong points, garrisons, airports, transportation centers, media locations and other known centers of gravity. The main center of gravity for all special operations forces was Noriega himself. He was so busy running, however, that he had little hand in directing the battle. Friendly centers of gravity employed were intelligence collection and joint communications and electronics. The rescue of prisoners was another center of gravity for the SOF as they impact the morale of both forces. The use of light armored vehicles provided the speed and mobility on the Panamanian roads that was critical to success of the operations as well.

Team Warfare was essential to success of Operation JUST CAUSE. US forces demonstrated their advanced training and readiness prior to receiving the alert order. The forces had learned much form lessons learned from other operations. They had more information due to the constant news stories that came out of Panama to better help them prepare mentally for the mission. Each commander had the advantage of detailed knowledge of the enemy through continuing intelligence collection and modern technology. General Thurman used the advantages of a foothold in the country to support the long operational reach provided by modern airdrop, logistics, and communications. The use of economy of force was brought to bear on critical centers of gravity during the strike by prioritizing objectives. This enabled mass to overwhelm critical points and centers of gravity. Other enemy critical items that were centers of gravity was five PDF installations and the Madden Dam which was important because it provided the electrical power to operate the Panama Canal.[35] Operation JUST CAUSE demonstrated that critical principles of war—objective, offensive, mass, economy of force, maneuver, security, surprise, and simplicity—bring victory today just as they did on other battlefields

Surprise plays a much greater role in strategy than in tactics. Also as stated by Clausewitz that in any specific action, in any measure we may undertake, we always have the choice between the most audacious and the most careful solution. Some people think that the theory of war always advises the latter. That assumption is false. If the theory does advise anything, it is the nature of war to advise the most decisive, that is, the most audacious. Theory leaves it to the military leader, however, to act according to his own courage, according to his spirit of enterprise, and his self-confidence. Make your choice, therefore, according to this inner force; but never forget that no military leader has ever become great without audacity.[36]

---

[35] JP 3-0, Chp. IV, p. IV-1 to IV-9.
[36] Clausewitz, Carl von (1942). Principles of War- Carl Von Clausewitz. The Military Service Publishing Company

Somalia

The American mission in Somalia presented the U.S. forces with a variety of difficult operational challenges as they tried to bring peace to a country ravaged by natural and man-made disasters. After initial success in the summer of 1992 in restoring order and saving thousands of lives, American soldiers clashed with Somalia forces and were withdrawn in the spring of 1994.[37] Listed are the following lessons learned:

TOPIC: Center of Gravity

DISCUSSION: Commanders must find the "Center of Gravity" for the operation. What is the single most important event or condition that will stabilize the situation and reverse the destruction and strife? During Operation RESTORE HOPE in Somalia, it was the opening of roads and the establishment of freedom of movement for the people. This allowed the relief agencies to distribute food to the starving people. The problem with operations other than war is that the commander may not be able to identify the "center of gravity" and its connection to the end state until the operation is well underway. If the purpose of peace enforcement is to bring about a political solution to a problem, the legitimacy of the force is the center of gravity. By ensuring the support of world opinion, including the begrudging acceptance by the parties that the force has a right to be there and is acting properly, the diplomatic resolution of the conflict is facilitated.[38]

---

[37] Allard, Kenneth (1995, January). Somalia Operations: Lessons Learned, Allard, National Defense University Press, Washington, DC, Forward.
[38] Ch IV, Notes for commanders—cog.

Terrorism

Dr. David Jablonsky, Professor of National Security Affairs at the Army War College, posits that the current challenge is to understand the role of both change and continuity in the dual aftermath of the end of the Cold War and a great military victory in the Persian Gulf War. The seeming end to the threat posed by the East-West confrontation of the past fifty years notwithstanding, the international community still looks to the United States, the world s only superpower, for leadership. But, argues Dr. Jablonsky, the U.S. military is caught between having to trim its size and force structure on the one hand, while preparing for a plethora of nontraditional missions on the other. Dr. Jablonsky makes the case that despite the vastly changed world order, basic principles of international relations still apply, and the United States would be ill-served by abandoning those principles. The current U.S. national security strategy and its derivative national military strategy are, indeed, products of change and continuity resulting from the dynamics established in inter-state relations over the past fifty years as well as by the end of the Cold War. For whatever else may have changed, national security remains the primary duty of the nation-state and the responsibility for achieving that mission still belongs to the military.[39]

As long as terrorist groups continue to target American citizens and interests, the United States will need to have specialized military units available to defeat such groups. From time to time, we might also find it necessary to strike terrorists at their bases abroad or to attack assets valued by the governments that support them. U.S. policy in countering international terrorists is to make no concessions to terrorists, continue to pressure state sponsors of terrorism, fully exploit all available legal mechanisms to punish international terrorists and help other

---

39 Time S Cycle and National Military Strategy, June 1, 1995.

governments improve their capabilities to combat terrorism. Countering terrorism effectively requires close, day-to-day coordination among Executive Branch agencies. Under the Clinton Administration, the efforts of the Departments of State, Justice and Defense, the FBI and CIA have been coordinated, with increased funding and manpower focused on the problem.

Positive results will come from integration of intelligence, diplomatic and rule-of-law activities, and through close cooperation with other governments and international counterterrorist organizations. Improving U.S. intelligence capabilities is a significant part of the U.S. response, as the evolving nature of the threat presents new challenges to the intelligence community. Terrorists, whether from well-organized groups or the kind of more loosely organized group responsible for the World Trade Center bombing, have the advantage of being able to take the initiative in the timing and choice of targets. Terrorism involving weapons of mass destruction represents a particularly dangerous potential threat that must be countered. The United States has made concerted efforts to punish and deter terrorists. On June 26, 1993, following a determination that Iraq had plotted an assassination attempt against former President Bush, President Clinton ordered a cruise missile attack against the headquarters of Iraq's intelligence service in order to send a firm response and deter further threats. Similarly, the United States obtained convictions against defendants in the bombing of the World Trade Center. In the last three years, more terrorists have been arrested and extradited to the United States than during the totality of the previous three Administrations. America was still determined to apprehend many others, including the suspected perpetrators of the Pan Am 103 bombing who was being sheltered in Libya, and those involved in the deadly attack on U.S. Government employees at CIA Headquarters in 1994. A growing number of nations have responded to the Administrations message urging international cooperation in the fight against terrorism. Ssuccess in hunting down terrorists is in large measure due to a growth of international intelligence sharing and increased international law enforcement efforts. At the Halifax Summit in 1995, the heads of state from the G-7 and Russia agreed to work more closely in combating terrorism. This led to the December 1995 ministerial in Ottawa, which announced a P-8 pledge to adopt all current counterterrorism treaties by the year 2000, to cooperate more closely in detecting forged documents and strengthening border surveillance, to share information more fully and effectively and to work together in preventing the use by terrorists of nuclear, biological and chemical weapons.

Iran's support of terrorism is a primary threat to peace in the Middle East and a major threat to innocent citizens everywhere. The President is determined to step up U.S. efforts bringing international pressure to bear on Iran for its support of terrorism. President Clinton imposed an embargo against Iran, depriving it of the benefits of trade and investment with the United States. The embargo's immediate effect was to further disrupt an Iranian economy already reeling from mismanagement, corruption and stagnant oil prices. The United States also has sought the support of our friends and allies to adopt policies to limit Teheran's threatening behavior. The G-7 has joined us in condemning

Iran's support for terrorism, and we have secured commitments from Russia and other members of the post-COCOM "Wassenaar Arrangement" export control regime not to sell weapons to Iran that have sensitive, dual-use technologies with military end-uses. U.S. leadership and close coordination with other governments and international bodies will continue, as also demonstrated by the UN Security Council sanctions against Libya for the Pan Am 103 and UTA 772 bombings, an international convention dealing with detecting and controlling plastic explosives, and two important counterterrorism treaties—the Protocol for the Suppression of Unlawful Acts of Violence at Airports Serving International Aviation and the Convention for the Suppression of Unlawful Attacks Against the Safety of Maritime Navigation.[40] The goal is to deal with terrorists and terrorist networks and the countries that are harboring those terrorist networks all across the United States and the world. Al Qaeda, as one example of a terrorist network, has 50 or 60 different cells in 50 or 60 different countries. So it is a big problem.[41]

Stunned by the magnitude of September 11, terrorist attacks, Congress and the White House reassessed an approach to fighting terrorism that favored the tools of law enforcement over those of war. The immediate focus of the discussions is President Bush's request for congressional authority to wage war on nontraditional foes such as Osama bin Laden, the top suspect in the attacks, and Afghanistan's ruling Taliban militia, which gives him refuge. In addition, outside experts have suggested that the administration set up a military tribunal that could try suspected terrorists outside the normal constraints of American constitutional law. In substance as well as tone—lawmakers and administration officials have referred often to "an act of war"—the debate over how to respond to the attacks appears to herald a significant shift in the nation's strategy for coping with terrorism. Beginning with the first Bush administration, policymakers have preferred to pursue terrorists through the courts. That was the strategy in the 1988 bombing of a Pan Am jetliner over Scotland and in the assault a decade later on two U.S. embassies in East Africa, both of which led to trials and convictions.

Although military force has always been an option—President Bill Clinton launched cruise missiles at Afghanistan and Sudan after the

---

[40] (1996). 1996 National Security Strategy. The White House.
[41] Rumsfeld, Donald H. (2001, October). DoD New Secretary Rumsfield Interview with Voice of America. DefenseLink.

embassy bombings—policymakers frequently have argued that such action only invites retaliation. The goal in treating terrorism as a criminal matter, a senior Clinton administration official said in an interview last year, is to "depoliticize" terrorism and "delegitimize" it in the eyes of the world. That legalistic approach has long had its critics, who say that putting terrorists on trial does not adequately address the role of hostile foreign governments, such as Libya or Iran, in sponsoring terrorism. They also say it complicates the work of intelligence agencies that may be inhibited by courtroom rules of evidence and procedure. Some saw vindication for their views in September 11, 2001 carnage. "The U.S. had judicialized more aspects of human behavior than any civilization in history, and may have come to the limit of that," said Stewart Baker, who served as general counsel to the National Security Agency from 1992 to 1994. "Frankly, if Osama bin Laden did this, he stated, I'm not really interested in bringing him back for a trial, and I don't think we're obliged to think in those terms." Daniel Benjamin, a counterterrorism specialist in the Clinton White House, said such arguments posit a "false choice" between a military and legal response to terrorism. "To be able to try someone under the laws of our society is an expression of the power of those laws," he said. " Having said that, military action is absolutely indicated in a situation like this if it can be effective." Benjamin acknowledged that "after an event like September 11, there has to be a fundamental shift" in how the nation defends itself against terrorism. And judging by the rhetoric, that shift has begun.

International organized crime jeopardizes the global trend toward peace and freedom, undermines fragile new democracies, saps the strength from developing countries and threatens our efforts to build a safer, more prosperous world. The rise of organized crime in the new independent states of the former Soviet Union and Central Europe weakens new democracies and poses a direct threat to U.S. interests, particularly in light of the potential for the theft and smuggling by organized criminals of nuclear materials left within some of these nations.

The Administration has launched a major initiative to combat international organized crime. Criminal enterprises are presently moving vast sums of illegal gains through the international financial system with impunity. In addition to invoking the International Emergency Economic Powers Act to undercut the financial underpinnings of criminal enterprises, the President has ordered an action plan to combat money laundering throughout the globe by directing the government to identify and put on notice nations that tolerate money laundering.

We intend to work with these nations to bring their banks and financial systems into conformity with the international standards against moneylaundering—or we will consider sanctions. The Justice Department is also drafting legislation, which will be submitted to Congress, to provide U.S. agencies with the tools they need to respond to organized criminal activity. Because the threat of organized crime comes from abroad as well as at home, we will work with other nations to keep our citizens safe. The President's invitation at the United Nations to all countries to join the United States in fighting international organized crime by measures of their own and by negotiating and endorsing an international declaration on citizens' safety—a declaration which would include a "no-sanctuary for organized criminals" pledge—is an effort to enhance our international cooperative efforts to protect our people.[42]

In his address to the nation on September 11, Bush vowed that "we will make no distinction between the terrorists who committed these acts and those who harbor them"—a point that has been echoed repeatedly on Capitol Hill. Lawmakers were not prepared to grant

---

[42] (1996). 1996 National Security Strategy. The White House.

Bush's initial request for unrestricted authority to wage war, fearing that such a resolution could return to haunt them if things turned sour, according to congressional staff members. Nevertheless, said a Senate aide, "the lawyers on both sides are sitting down to try to figure out what needed to be done to give the president all the authority he felt he needed," while retaining an oversight role for Congress. Some former law enforcement officials close to the Bush administration suggest that the government set up a military tribunal to deal with terrorism suspects who are apprehended or turned over to U.S. authorities. "A tribunal is a civilized response that lies between just killing the perpetrators and giving them the full panoply of rights afforded to U.S. citizens in U.S. courts," said Charles Cooper, a former high-ranking Justice official during the Reagan administration. "Civil courts would not be an appropriate forum for those prosecuting war against our country." A source confirmed that the White House is considering the possibility that Bush could establish such a tribunal or ask Congress to do so.

"The Constitution is intended to protect the liberties of American people, not terrorists overseas," said a former senior law enforcement official.

"Prosecuting these people in U.S. courts doesn't make any sense if you're essentially in a state of war." There were some precedent for a swift and harsh response to terrorist attack. In 1986, President Ronald Reagan launched air raids against the Libyan capital of Tripoli, killing 39 people, days after the bombing of a Berlin discotheque in which two American servicemen died. U.S. intelligence had pinned the bombing on Libya. Libya was also identified as the primary culprit in the Dec. 21, 1988, bombing of Pan Am Flight 103 over Lockerbie, Scotland, which killed 270 people. But that attack triggered a more cautious American response, in part because U.S. intelligence did not reach its conclusion about Libyan involvement until more than a year later. U.S. officials also feared that a military response would do nothing to enhance national security—and, in fact, might goad Libya's erratic leader, Moammar Gaddafi, into further attacks on U.S. interests. So the Bush administration opted for the criminal justice route, indicting the two Libyan suspects and insisting that Libya turn them over for trial.

Under pressure of U.N. economic sanctions, Libya finally did so in 1999; one of them was convicted this year by a Scottish court in the Netherlands. William Barr, attorney general in the first Bush administration, had asked the Scots to consider setting up a joint military tribunal, but they declined.[43]

In an address by Secretary Colin Powell he stated that America's leadership of a global coalition, here in this crisis with the Taliban and with al-Qaida and Usama bin Laden and terrorism, America's leadership of the global campaign against this kind of threat to civilization, this kind of threat to the very essence of what you do, taking care of people, it is terrorism that is directed against people; it represents no faith, no religion. It is evil, it is murderous. That's why the word "terrorism" fits this, and that's why the word "terrorist" is the right noun to apply to people like Usama bin Laden. And the United States with a grand coalition is responding to this 21st century challenge. The U.S. was exerting leadership, but was working with a wide range of others, both traditional partners and allies, as well as new ones, including those willing to move beyond past animosities to reach new shared goals. Already, in forming the anti-terrorism coalition, we have revitalized alliances and we have worked with the United Nations and with regional organizations representing the entire globe to leverage strength. And we have opened doors to qualitatively different relationships with a number of countries that we might not have thought of having such relationships just a few years

---

[43] Lancaster, Jon , & Schmidt, Susan (2001, September). U_S_ Rethinks Strategy for copying with terrorist. The Washington Post Online. www.washingtonpost.com/ac2/wp-dyn?

ago. Collectively, the international community is taking crucial steps to share information, improve security through greater cooperation by working with law enforcement agencies in all of these countries, intelligence agencies, and financial agencies, to cut off the financial lifeline that terrorism depends upon.

In this global campaign, the United States welcomes the help of any country or any party that is genuinely prepared to work with us. For we will not relax our standards, and we will not abandon our principled interests in human rights, accountable government, free markets, nonproliferation, conflict resolution. We believe that a world of democracy, a world of opportunity, a world of stability is a world in which terrorism cannot thrive.[44]

In the meantime, the U.S. military will continue to plan for uncertainty in the best tradition of Admiral Horatio Nelson. But in case signals can neither be seen or perfectly understood, the admiral instructed off Cadiz in October 1805, no captain can do very wrong if he places his ship alongside that of an enemy.

The problem today is that even the enemy ships are not yet clearly visible, leaving U.S. planners to face the adverse confluence of both Time s Cycle and Arrow. Times Cycle begins with Edward Gibbon s reminder that history is indeed little more than the register of the crimes, follies, and misfortunes of mankind. Historical experience also suggests that by the time a distant threat emerges as a clear and present danger to the United States, it will be too late, as it was in 1941 when the Imperial Japanese Navy had to announce that danger from the air. At the same time, the ongoing unprecedented technological revolution in Times Arrow is creating an increasingly more instantaneously dangerous

---

[44] Powell, Colin L. (2001, October). Remarks to the National Foreign Policy Conference For Leaders of NGOs, October 26, 2001. U.S. Department of State. www.state.gov/secretary/rm/2001/index.cfm?docid=5762

world. In such an environment, capabilities planning will form the basis for threat-based requirements planning and implementation when it is needed in the future. On the other hand, a return in the present to threat-based requirements planning can lead to a new version of the Ten Year Rule, in which even the existence of Nelson s enemy ships is assumed away. It is in this context that the National Military Strategy of the United States ultimately plays its most important role. The JCS document clearly underscores the need for a selective and flexible strategy in the calculation of the relationship between the means, the BUR force, and the ends, the thwarting of aggression and the promotion of stability. That emphasis is demonstrated throughout the national military strategy in the focus on the use of all elements of national power to achieve the overarching twin objectives and on the great care that the United States must exercise in using military forces as instruments of national policy. The strategy also reflects the iterative interaction of the JCS with the NCA, a relationship reflected in the President s national security strategy and the Defense Secretary s annual report. Equally important, the document provides the Chairman a single, unclassified outlet to make his case for the controlled build-down of U.S. military forces in protecting and opportunistically extending the current transition. In making that case, the national military strategy also demonstrates that capabilities-based planning is not synonymous with a military effort to collectively feather its organizational nest. National security for the strategic hedgehog is the ultimate duty of the nation-state; and even in the vast complexities of the modern world, the primary responsibility for achieving that mission still belongs to the military. In the end, that reminder may be the most important rationale for continuing to publish the unclassified national military strategy document.[45]

---

[45] Jablonsky, David (1995, June). Time S Cycle and National Military Strategy. www.dtic.mil/doctrine/jcl/research_pubs/timecycle.pdf.

Nearly 55 years ago, in his final inaugural address, President Franklin Delano

Roosevelt reflected on the lessons of the first half of the 20th Century. "We have learned," he said, "that we cannot live alone at peace. We have learned that our own well being is dependent on the well being of other nations far away. We have learned to be citizens of the world, members of the human community." Those words have more reso-nance than ever as we enter the 21st century. America is at the height of its influence and prosperity. But, at a time of rapid globalization, when events halfway around the earth can profoundly affect our safety and prosperity, America must lead in the world to protect our people at home and our way of life. Americans benefit when nations come together to deter aggression and terrorism, to resolve conflicts, to pre-vent the spread of dangerous weapons, to promote democracy and human rights, to open markets and create financial stability, to raise liv-ing standards, to protect the environment - to face challenges that no nation can meet alone.

The United States remains the world's most powerful force for peace, prosperity and the universal values of democracy and freedom. Our nation's central challenge—and our responsibility—is to sustain that role by seizing the opportunities of this new global era for the benefit of our own people and people around the world. To do that, we are pursu-ing a forward-looking national security strategy for the new century.

Military leaders have seen encouraging signs that America has turned the corner on readiness. Although our Armed Forces still face readiness challenges, particularly in recruiting and retaining skilled individuals, Administration initiatives are helping us achieve our readiness goals. America's military is—and will continue to be—capable of carrying out national strategy and meeting America's defense commitments around the world. American leadership will remain indispensable to further important national interests in the coming year; forging a lasting peace in the Middle East; securing the peace in the Balkans and Northern Ireland; helping Russia strengthen its economy and fight corruption as it heads toward its first democratic transfer of power; furthering arms control through discussions with Russia on the Anti-Ballistic Missile (ABM) Treaty and deeper reductions in strategic nuclear weapons; implementing China's entry into the WTO and other global institutions while promoting freedom and human rights there; easing tensions between India and Pakistan; building on hopeful developments between Greece and Turkey to make progress in the Aegean, particularly on Cyprus; securing new energy routes from the Caspian Sea that will allow newly independent states in the Caucasus to prosper; supporting democratic transitions from Nigeria to Indonesia; helping Colombia defeat the drug traffickers who threaten its democracy; fighting weapons proliferation, terrorism and the nexus between them; restraining North Korea's and Iran's missile programs; maintaining vigilance against Iraq and working to bring about a change in regime; consolidating reforms to the world's financial architecture as the basis for sustained economic growth; launching a new global trade round; enacting legislation to promote trade with Africa and the Caribbean; pressing ahead with debt relief for countries fighting poverty and embracing good government; reversing global climate change; and protecting our oceans. At this moment in history, the United States is called upon to lead—to marshal the forces of freedom and progress; to channel the energies of the global economy into lasting prosperity; to reinforce our democratic ideals and values; to enhance American security and global peace. We owe it to our children and grandchildren to meet these challenges and build a better and safer world.[46]

---

[46] (1999, December). U_S_Dept_of State—IIP U_S_ commitment: A National Strategy for a new Century. White House, Office of Press Secretary.

On January 5, the White House released a 71-page report entitled, "A National Security Strategy for a New Century." This report is required by a Defense Department reorganization law passed in 1986. The document preface states "we are pursuing a forward- looking national security strategy for the new century. This report...sets forth that strategy. Its three core objectives are: To enhance America's security. To bolster America's economic prosperity. To promote democracy and human rights abroad." The report does not have a separate section on defense science and technology. There are many security objectives that identified in the report that have an important technological component, such as arms control. Beyond those areas, there are the following passages on defense: In a section entitled "Advancing U.S. National Interests", under the heading "Military Activities": "We are committed to maintaining U.S. leadership in space. Unimpeded access to and use of space is a vital national interest—essential for protecting U.S. national security, promoting our prosperity and ensuring our well-being. . . We will maintain our technological superiority in space systems, and sustain a robust U.S. space industry and a strong, forward-looking research base. We also will continue efforts to prevent the spread of weapons of mass destruction to space, and will continue to pursue global partnerships addressing space-related scientific, economic, environmental and security issues." In the same section, under a heading "Preparing for an Uncertain Future": "We must prepare for an uncertain future even as we address today's security problems. We need to look closely at our national security apparatus to ensure its effectiveness by adapting its institutions to meet new challenges. This means we must transform our capabilities and organizations—diplomatic, defense, intelligence, law enforcement, and economic—to act swiftly and to anticipate new opportunities and threats in today's continually evolving, highly complex international security environment. Preparing for an uncertain future also means that we must have a

strong, competitive, technologically superior, innovative and responsive industrial and research and development base."

Later under this same heading: "Transformation of our military
forces is critical to meeting the military challenges of the next century.
Exploiting the revolution in military affairs is fundamental if U.S. forces
are to retain their dominance in an uncertain world. Investment in
research and development while closely monitoring trends in likely
future threats are important elements of our transformation effort. A
carefully planned and focused modernization program will maintain
our technological superiority and replace Cold War-era equipment
with new systems and platforms capable of supporting the full spectrum of military operations. "Transformation extends well beyond the
acquisition of new military systems—we seek to leverage technological,
doctrinal, operational and organizational innovations to give U.S.
forces greater capabilities and flexibility."

Under another heading entitled "Enhancing American Competitiveness":
"Technological advantage. We will continue to support a vigorous science
and technology base that promotes economic growth, creates high-wage
jobs, sustains a healthy, educated citizenry, and provides the basis for our
future military systems. We will invest in education and training to develop a
workforce capable of participating in our rapidly changing economy. And we
will invest in world-class transportation, information and space infrastruc-
tures for the twenty-first century."[47]

To sum it up, General Montgomery C. Meigs, addressing a 2000
Kermit Roosevelt Lecturer in the United Kingdom, best stated the
changing times. He stated in his address the following insights:

---

[47] Jones, Richard M. (2000, January). White House Releases National
Security Strategy Report. The American Institute of Physics Bulletin of
Science Policy News.

We find ourselves in "interesting times", because we are experiencing a shift in the nature of the art of operations. We must adapt our understanding of the art of operations and also challenge to hold onto the relevant aspects of classic theory of operational art.

The realities of the information age are changing the operational environment in fundamental ways. We get it quicker and detect it easier. This is demanding new rules for how soldiers must do their business.

The paradigm shift goes beyond simply the new possibilities of information technology. There will be more commitment of forces, in joint formations, and in combined or multinational ones.

We will be operating on ca complex battlefield that combines the challenges of difficult and unfamiliar terrain, terrorists, and paramilitaries, and refugees and unfriendly civilian organizations.

We will still need to apply an overwhelming force against the enemy's operational center of gravity in order to win quickly at least cost.[48]

---

[48] Montgomery, Meigs, C.. Gen, Operational Art in the New Century, Parameters, Spring 2001, pp. 4–14.

Chapter 4

Summary

Basic to the proposed study of the development and growth of the United States Military Operational Strategy, first a review of how some feel the National Command Authority's acceptance of Isolationism may be the cause of our current crisis with terrorism. Second, a critical appraisal of Center of Gravity by leading experts as they attempt to define center of gravity, decision points, and vulnerability will serve to focus this study and provide any guidance the authorities give in determining center of gravity as well as look at any distinction they make between strategic and operational centers of gravity. Finally an analysis will be done to determine the center of gravity of the Gulf War, Panama Operation, Somalia Operation and the current war on terrorism to further illuminate this study. Hence, the U. S. Military must develop a universally accepted Joint understanding of center of gravity in order transition into its new doctrine and to defeat terrorism.

About the Author

Dr., CPT Joseph W. Graham received his Ph. D., MBA, and BBA degree in Business Administration. He currently lives in Atlanta, GA and is a career military officer in the United States Army. You can find other works by the author at www.Totalpowervictories.com.

0-595-22259-5